# SCRUMS, LINEOUTS & TRIES

## RUGBY UNION - AMERICA'S NEWEST, OLDEST GAME

By JON PASSMORE

Scrums, Lineouts & Tries

Rugby Union - America's Newest, Oldest Game

©2023, Jon Passmore

ISBN: 978-1-66788-740-1

ISBN eBook: 978-1-66788-741-8

# ACKNOWLEDGEMENTS

Any enterprise that involves writing a book about an international sport from the perspective of two countries thousands of miles apart is going to need a lot of help and I have had an abundance of support; numerous people have provided me with information, opinion, and a lot of good ideas.

A connection with **Rugby School** in England was an obvious place to start and my heartfelt thanks go out to my friend, former colleague and Old Rugbeian, **Tom Chadwick** and the staff at the school, including **Kerry Wilson** (former Director of Development), **Jennifer Hunt** (Archivist Manager), **Vicky Henderson** (Events Coordinator), **Liselle Dixon** (Rugbeian Community Assistant), **Mike Bayly** (Director of Rugby) and **Julie Morton** and **AnnaMaria Smith** at the School BookStore. I must also thank the young ladies of **Griffin House** and their Housemistress, **Liz Robinson** who welcomed and entertained me to lunch during a fascinating day at the School.

The Old Rugbeian network has significant contacts in the US and **Charles Cockerton** has been extremely helpful in connecting me to some highly engaged people in the US including **Jo Healey**, Executive Director of the British American Business Council in

Northern California, who shared some of her deep connections in the rugby network.

My research into the state of American rugby today led me to long conversations with **Marc Downes**, former professional rugby player in the UK and current assistant coach at Yale University and **Tony Ridnell**, a former USA Eagles team member and devotee of growing the game. **Todd Clever**, holder of a record 100 caps representing the USA at rugby sevens and fifteens and now Director of Strategic Partnerships at the **LA Giltinis** offered fascinating insight into the workings of America's relatively new professional game. **Tom Billups**, the Associate Head Coach at **University of California Berkeley's** highly successful rugby team was extremely generous in describing the successes and challenges faced by the college game and showed me the terrific facilities available to America's top flight collegiate athletes.

Of course, not all budding athletes get to go to America's finest universities and it was encouraging to hear about the growing network of rugby opportunities available to young players around the country. Several organizations are promoting and funding inner-city rugby for under-privileged kids: **Wil Snape-Rogers** at **Play Rugby USA** shared a lot of information about this corner of the rugby "development" market; **Stuart Bagshaw**, Member of the Board of Trustees of the **Atlas Foundation** described how his organization raises awareness and funds such opportunities for young kids to play, belong and thrive.

**Brad Dufresne**, President of the **New England Rugby Football Union** helped me understand the workings of club rugby in this vast country both from his position at the helm of a regional organization but also through his club, the **Monadnock RFC** in Keene, NH.

I had the good fortune to speak to some of the giants of the contemporary game including **Chris Robshaw,** former England Captain and holder of 66 caps for his country, **Simon Shaw**, also of England fame (71 caps) and team member on three British and Irish Lions tours, and **Shane Byrne** (41 caps for ireland and 4 appearance for the Lions). From these highly experienced players comes the wisdom of context, not only about their own playing experience, but what it takes to grow the game, individually and collectively, and reach a high, global standard.

Arguably, the leaders of **USARugby** have an enormous task ahead of them, especially with World Cup host nation responsibilities in 2031 and 2033. It was enlightening to meet with the CEO, **Ross Young** and COO, **Jonathan Atkeison** at this early stage of the organization's journey.

**Dave Saward,** a highly successful D3 soccer coach at **Middlebury College** in VT for over 30 years introduced me to the power of parents, coaches and organisers and the importance of their support, especially in contact sports, and **Rob Bonnet**, long-time sports analyst, commentator and journalist for **BBC TV and Radio** provided wisdom on the art of communication in the rarified air of global sporting competition.

On a practical note, I was helped in my journey to write a book by **Tom Connor**, a rugby enthusiast and literary expert; **Geoffrey Norman**, master of the red pen and matters grammatical; **Jack**

**Schofield** who offered his artistic flair to the finished product and **Britta Stratton** for her flattering photography.

Finally, my thanks go out to my family, especially my wife, Carol who has mixed feelings about rugby, but has tolerated my incessant tapping on a laptop, and joined me at games in LA and Berkeley with good humor and patience. I am forever grateful to her and our two sons, **William and Matthew**; they support me in everything I do.

My deepest thanks to everyone involved.

# CONTENTS

# FOREWORD

**"The Pen is mightier than the Sword, and is
considerably easier to write with."**

**Marty Feldman**

This book was written during the run-up to the quadrennial World
Cup tournament 2023, hosted by France, perhaps a good time to
offer an explanation of this global sport. A happy coincidence is
that this book will be available on the 200th anniversary of the birth
of rugby football, "created" by a young scholar at Rugby School in
England, in 1823.

While I hope all rugby fans will find enjoyment in these pages, the
primary target is people who are looking at rugby seriously for the
first time. They may be potential players, coaches or the parents
of boys and girls who have an opportunity to play the game. They
may be sports fans for whom rugby is a new adventure, drawn by
the intense enthusiasm shown for the sport in many countries
around the world. But whoever you are, I hope you will feel the
**passion** I have for this game; the **gratitude** I feel for the players,
coaches, referees, supporters and administrators who arrange our

entertainment week-in, week-out; my **admiration** for a game that can be so physically uncompromising yet so strict in its exercise of fair play and respect; and **delight** in how rugby creates community engagement, especially in the grass-roots clubs and villages where the game developed.

My qualifications for writing this book come from my love for the game, from a lifetime of watching the game, playing as a young kid and refereeing later in life. Seeing the passion exhibited both on and off the pitch on miserable, wet days in darkest Kent, or hearing the roar of 82,000 fans at Twickenham Stadium in southwest London, England's temple of rugby. Watching players at the pinnacle of the game, pushing themselves to greater heights, and observing the friendship and their respect for each other, after 80 minutes of action that would make a warrior flinch. Unforgettable memories.

The purpose of this book is to educate in terms that make sense and foster enjoyment, providing endless talking points for enthusiasts over a pint or a cup of tea after no-side has been called.

I hope you enjoy it.

Jon Passmore

# PART ONE
# "THE GAME"

WILLIAM WEBB ELLIS

WHO WITH A FINE DISREGARD FOR THE RULES OF
FOOTBALL AS PLAYED IN HIS TIME
FIRST TOOK THE BALL IN HIS ARMS AND RAN
WITH IT THUS ORIGINATING THE DISTINCTIVE
FEATURE OF THE RUGBY GAME
AD 1823

The William Webb Ellis plaque at Rugby School, England

# RUGBY UNION

**"I do love cricket - it's so very English."**

**Sarah Bernhardt watching a game of football**

Life is confusing, just ask Sarah Bernhardt.

Think of this as a guide book, a reference manual for people who:

    a. are thinking about playing or coaching the game and want to know what they're letting themselves in for;

    b. are parents of a girl or boy who wants to play rugby and want to reassure themselves about this complex sport;

    c. may not want to play the game but would like to referee it;

    d. are fans of sport in general but don't know much about the game and want to learn.

To satisfy the concerns of these constituents in a book that is both interesting and portable requires a pretty broad brush. This book will provide the parent, the embryonic player, the enthusiast or just the curious, with a guide to rugby in all its glory, providing a solid introduction to the game of scrums and lineouts, rucks and mauls and five-eighths and locks, and a bit more besides.

Rugby is an international sport and, at the highest level, fields teams from Europe, Africa, Australasia, Asia and South America. Missing from this list is North America and I confess that part of my motivation for writing this book has been a desire to see the game grow in the consciousness of American athletes and communities.

The book introduces you to the game of rugby in three sections:

**The Game** itself, taking a look at the fundamentals of the sport and the support functions that surround it;

**The Foundations of the Game** - how it started, where it is today and what it needs to thrive in America;

**Rugby's Culture**, covering the Ethos and Laws that govern this complex sport, Referees and, most importantly, Health and Safety, critical to its long-term success.

First of all, let's look at the basics of the game: how it is played; who plays it; and explain some of the terms and expressions that are heard in the rugby world. It has a language all of its own, and after reading this book, you'll be speaking fluent rugby!

# 1 - FUNDAMENTALS

## TEAMWORK - RESPECT - ENJOYMENT- DISCIPLINE - SPORTSMANSHIP

**Winston Churchill, when asked what he thought about American Football replied, "Actually, it is somewhat like Rugby. But why do you have all those committee meetings?"**

(In the next two chapters, if any terms and colloquialisms are confusing, please refer to Chapter 2 for an explanation of these expressions.)

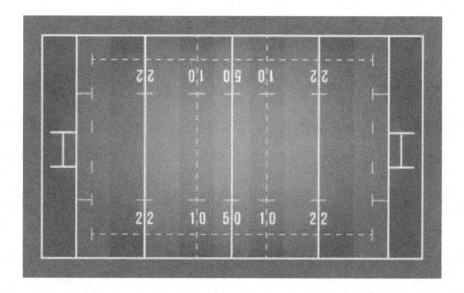

## The pitch

Rugby Union is played by two teams of 15 players, The game is played on a large, rectangular playing surface (the field of play) approximately 100 meters by 60 meters with tall goal posts at each end. Behind those posts is the "in-goal" area where the ball must be touched down to score a try (worth 5 points). Additional points can be scored by kicking the ball between the posts and above the crossbar, thereby converting the try, for 2 points or scoring a penalty or drop goal for 3 points.

Several lines both along and across the field of play include locations for restarting the game, holding lineouts and identifying a defending team's 22 meter line where additional rules apply.

## The purpose

The objective is to score more points than the opponent through tries, conversions and penalties and each team comprises two types of players: larger, heavier, stronger folk whose job is in the set pieces (scrums and lineouts) and breakdown (after a tackle), where possession may be gained; and faster but nonetheless strong and athletic types whose job it is to run with the ball and score. In the modern professional game, the body types and capabilities of these players have become more similar - total rugby demands strength, speed and ball-handling from each of the 15 players. As a result, an increasing number of players on the team are capable of, and do score tries.

After each score, the team that conceded the points restarts the game by kicking off at the halfway line into their opponent's territory. The competition for possession of the ball resumes.

The teams play two halves of 40 minutes with a 10 or 15 minute break in between. The game is controlled by a referee and two touch judges/assistant referees. For professional and international games, a fourth official is provided (a television match official or TMO) who can assist the referee with tough calls sometimes obscured by the speed of play and the frequent presence of very large bodies.

# UNIQUE ASPECTS OF RUGBY

- The ball is passed between the players by hand and must be passed parallel to the line of play or backwards to avoid an infringement

- Kicking is important, both tactically for field position, and for scoring points (conversions, penalties and drop-goals)

- Tackling any player not in possession of the ball is prohibited

- Tackling must involve the arms (wrapping)

- Referees will use the Advantage Law aggressively to avoid unnecessary stoppages in play

- Players can receive a yellow card (10 minutes in the Sin Bin) for offenses ranging from slowing the game to dangerous play. In extreme cases (repeated infringements by a player or danger to an opponent) a red card may be issued, compelling the player to leave the field of play for the remainder of the match, with potential for further sanctions.

- Substitutions are permanent, except in the case of: excessive bleeding when a player may leave the field for stitches; or Head Injury Assessments, when a player has received a heavy knock and requires examination by a medical professional.

The rules of the game are designed to encourage continuous play where both sides are offered multiple, fair opportunities to contest for the ball. Time-wasting and Oscar-worthy acting-hurt behaviors are actively discouraged and inevitably attract the negative attention of the referee who has broad powers to dispense punishments. Above all, fair play and respect are hallmarks of the game.

The players on the team are identified by a unique number that signifies a particular position on the field.

# RUGBY POSITIONS

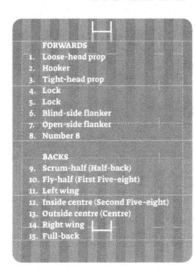

**FORWARDS**
1. Loose-head prop
2. Hooker
3. Tight-head prop
4. Lock
5. Lock
6. Blind-side flanker
7. Open-side flanker
8. Number 8

**BACKS**
9. Scrum-half (Half-back)
10. Fly-half (First Five-eight)
11. Left wing
12. Inside centre (Second Five-eight)
13. Outside centre (Centre)
14. Right wing
15. Full-back

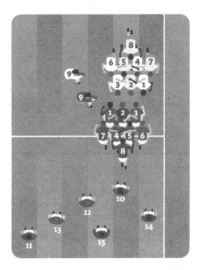

**The Scrum - the group within the team who are charged with winning the ball at set pieces (scrums and lineouts), carrying the ball for short distances, tackling the opposition and winning the ball at the breakdown,**

1 Loose-head Prop

2 Hooker

3 Tight head-Prop

4 Second row/Lock

5 Second row/ Lock

6 Blind-side Flanker/Wing Forward

7 Open-side Flanker/Wing Forward

8 Number Eight

**The Backs - the players responsible for using speed and agility to get past the opposition in attack, and defending deep in their own half, using their speed to launch counterattacks.**

9 Scrum Half

10 Fly Half/First Five-Eighth

11 Left Wing

12 Inside Center/Second Five-Eighth

13 Outside Center

14 Right Wing

15 Full Back

Teams can have up to 8 substitutes (depending on the level of game played), numbered 16 to 23.

Note: Player's numbers are NEVER retired in Rugby: the player occupies the shirt number temporarily, hoping to leave it in a better place than when he or she found it.

# OTHER DISCIPLINES

This book focuses on 15-man Rugby Union, but there are other disciplines of rugby, including rugby league and **Rugby 7's**, recently reintroduced to the Olympic Games.in Rio (2016). The game is played on the same size pitch as the larger game emphasizing the need for a high level of speed, agility and stamina. ,


**"In 1823, William Webb Ellis first picked up the ball in his arms and ran with it. And for the next 156 years forwards have been trying to work out why."**

**Tasker Watkins, President of the Welsh Rugby Union**

# 2 - TERMS, EXPRESSIONS & COLLOQUIALISMS

"The limits of my language mean the limits of my world"

**Ludwig Wittgenstein**

Before delving any deeper into this book it would be helpful for you to acquire a basic understanding of the terms that will crop up in my explanations. This will also help in comprehending the laws of the game allowing you to:

1) enjoy watching or playing the game,

2) participate in the loud and generally good-natured public banter that makes spectating such a pleasure, and

3) avoid making a chump of yourself at a game, in a bar or when you send personal suggestions to the referee after the match.

The terms laid out below are NOT the laws as specifically defined by World Rugby – this segment is devoted to the unique words that occur in rugby which, when you know and understand them, will identify you as a true and serious fan of the game.

Rugby is not alone in this: every sport has its own colloquialisms, like bunt, pick and PAT (which, combined, sounds like a rather saucy game in and of itself) – words associated with 3 particular American sports – kudos if you get them right*.

Finally, the following rugby terms occurred to me somewhat at random and are not arranged in any order of importance or relevance to the game. They are, however, (largely) unique to rugby and have been developed over the many decades the game has been in existence:

# POSITIONS

## The Tight Five

**Front Row: Loose-head and Tight-head Props (#1 & 3)** – players in the front row of forwards, either side of the hooker, who connect with the opposing front row in a zipper-like fashion. The player whose head is on the outside is known as the loose-head prop and the player with opposing heads either side of his own is called the tight head.

**Front Row: Hooker (#2)** – the middle position in the front row of a scrum whose job it is to "hook" the ball backwards, with his feet, ensuring possession for his team. Also responsible for the throw-in at a lineout as he is often the shortest player on the team and, therefore, does not jump very high.

**Second row (# 4 & 5 – aka Locks, the engine room)** – two players of considerable height, weight and strength who add power to the push in the scrum. Key players in the line out where their height can be a crucial advantage.

## The Loose Forwards

**Flankers (# 6 & 7)** – the two players on either side of the scrum who are only "attached" to that heaving mass by one arm, giving them mobility and, therefore, opportunity. These big, fast players can quickly peel off the scrum once the ball is out and chase down opposing ball carriers or support their own teammates in attack.

**Number 8** – perched at the back of the scrum, this is a key tactical position. Large but mobile, the #8 is equally important in attack and defense and with the flankers can present a major threat to the opposition. Unlike the "tight five" (props, hooker and second row) who are physically entangled in the scrum, the positions 6, 7 and 8 are very mobile.

## (Numbers 1 - 8 are also known as "The Pack")

## The Half Backs

**Scrum Half (#9)** - the essential link between the pack and the three quarters, those speed-merchants who can run, bob and weave around the opposition and score tries. The scrum half collects the ball when it emerges from a set piece (scrum or lineout) and from the breakdown after a tackle, and distributes it appropriately: often to the waiting Fly Half. The enterprising 9 will make darting runs, ball in hand, to keep the opponents under pressure.

**Fly Half (#10)** - often the major tactician on the team, the 10 will receive the ball from the scrum half and instantly choose the best option for this phase of play - pass, kick or run with the ball. 10's are often the primary kicker, for position, penalties and conversions.

## The Three-Quarters

**Inside and Outside Centers (# 12 & 13)** - often taller and heavier but nonetheless very quick runners with the ball whose actions are designed to test the stoutness of the opposition defense.

**The Wings (#11 and 14)** - selected for speed and agility, these are the players whose value is realized in multiphase play when defenses become disorganized and gaps emerge to be exploited.

**The Full Back (#15)** - classically the last line of defense, modern 15s are always used in attack as an extra element to overwhelm stretched defenses. While every player needs to be adept at catching high balls, 15s are recognized as masters of this art.

[NOTE: the above emphasizes the offensive skills of these positions but defense, i.e tackling is a task that EVERY player must excel at.]

# DURING THE GAME

**The scrum** – an equal competition for the ball (although the side putting the ball in has the advantage) comprising two "packs" of eight forwards pushing against each other on the referee's command, in an attempt to overwhelm their opponents and gain possession of the ball.

A scrum occurs when a minor infringement has taken place and a team is given the advantage of a put in. The scrum half (#9) rolls the ball towards his side and the ball will be played, using the feet only, to the back of the scrum. On emerging from this heaving mass of humanity, the ball may be picked up and open play recommences.

**The loose** – when the ball has emerged from a set-piece (kick, scrum or lineout) and is flying about the field with both teams in hot pursuit, competing for possession – one looking to keep it and the other to capture it.

**The breakdown** – occurs when a player carrying the ball is tackled and the ball is momentarily up for grabs. Entering the breakdown, legally, quickly and aggressively can help the team in possession keep it, or the defending team to steal it.

**The Off-load** - a player with the ball, when tackled around the legs may have an opportunity to pass the ball to a colleague while falling to ground. Some top players are remarkably skilled at getting rid of the ball in seemingly impossible situations.

**The Jackal/Jackaler** - a player who "steals" the ball in the breakdown from an opposition player who has been tackled. Requiring tremendous strength and timing, these players can reverse the flow of a game in an instant.

**The ruck/counter-ruck** – basically an unorganized, spontaneous scrum that presents an equal opportunity event after a tackle. Comprises two or more players, on their feet with the ball on the ground between them. They may push against each other and use their feet (no hands!) to move the ball to the back of the ruck and the eager hands of their scrum half.

**The maul** – three or more players, one from each side and the player carrying the ball, all on their feet, wrestling for possession. When the referee announces that a maul has been formed, woe betide anyone who impedes progress by tripping an opponent or falling over (collapsing the maul). If the maul makes no progress downfield, the referee will call "Use It" to the scrum half who must do so within 5 seconds.

**A rolling maul** – as described above but where the attacking team (carrying the ball) makes considerable distance toward their opponents try line with the momentum that only 2,000 lbs. of sweating beef can provide. Again, if the defending team uses anything but sheer strength and technique to slow this progress, a penalty can be awarded.

**Phases** – when a team maintains possession despite multiple tackles, breakdowns, rucks and mauls, the sequence of play is measured in phases. Each cycle of run – tackle/breakdown – recycle, counts as a phase. Periods of play with high numbers of phases (with one team maintaining possession) are exciting to watch and exhausting to play against, requiring very high standards of fitness and technique.

**The lineout** – when the ball goes into touch (off the field of play, along the sidelines) at the hand (or foot) of one team, their opponent gets to throw it back in at the lineout. This consists of two lines of forwards, perpendicular to the touch line at the point where the ball left the field of play, the number of attendees (usually 5 - 7) being decided by the throwing team.

Note: the only times the ball is thrown in by the team who kicked the ball into touch are:

1) after a penalty and

2) Under the new 50/22 rule
   (See: The Laws: recent amendments)

**Referee calls at the scrum** – the most pertinent part of the Laws of rugby that pertain to the scrum are those that cover its operation and safety. The set-up of the scrum is crucial and attracts intense scrutiny from the referee. Given the colossal forces at work (this is where injuries can occur), the referees will chant a mantra of **"crouch"** (preparation), **"bind"** (the props grab their opponents' jerseys), "set" (the two teams come together). Any player who is lined up incorrectly or seeks to gain an unfair advantage by pushing early or at an angle will be punished.

**Against the head** – the side throwing the ball in at the line out and putting in at the scrum has a decisive advantage – they know when and where they are going to throw it. They deserve this advantage as the other team committed an offense against them. A win of the ball by the opposing team is called going "against the head" and provides a significant tactical and psychological victory.

# THE KICKING GAME

**Drop kicks** – where the ball touches the ground an instant before it is kicked. Used for the kick-off at the start of each half; for restarts after scores; for 22-Meter line and goal-line drop outs (more later); and for goal attempts in open play (3 points, if successful).

**Place kicks** – from a designated point on the ground, used for penalties when attempting a kick for goal and for conversions. A tee is used to remove the disadvantage of a rough, uneven field.

**Punts** – when the ball is kicked from hand (does not touch the ground). Used for kicking to touch for positional reasons and after penalties; for field position in the course of open play; and to challenge the opponent's defense with high "up and under" kicks in an attempt to force an error and gain possession downfield. When both teams challenge their opposite numbers with kicks downfield, it is known as "kick tennis" and can test the patience of the spectators.

**The 50:22 Rule** - when a player kicks, from inside his own half, and it bounces in the opponent's 22 (between the 22-Meter line and the goal line) before going out of play. When that occurs, the attacking side gets the throw-in, a major tactical advantage.

# SCORING

**The try** – the main objective of the game is to get points on the board and the try gains the largest score (5 pts). The ball must be carried over the try line into the "in goal" area and placed firmly on the ground. Downward pressure must be applied; a dropped ball does not count. The ball may also be kicked over the try line, be caught or picked up by an on-side teammate and touched down.

**The conversion** – the team that has just scored a try has the opportunity to increase their score by two points by place-kicking the ball (off the ground or a tee) from a spot on a line parallel to the touch line and in line with where the ball was touched down for the try. The kicker decides where to kick from, using commonsense, leg strength and basic trigonometry to aim the ball between the posts and above the bar of the goal at the end of the field where the try was scored.

**Penalty try** – a defending team subject to a relentless onslaught close to their try line may resort to desperate tactics to prevent a try being scored. If they stay within the laws, fine, but should they continuously disrupt play by lying on the ball or being persistently offside, the referee will get fed up and may award a penalty try to the attackers even if one has not been scored. A conversion is not needed, 7 points are awarded. In addition, the guilty player might be yellow- or red-carded depending on the severity of the offense.

# Additional, important rules on the field of play

**Knock-on** – passing the ball forward in rugby is illegal and strictly forbidden. If, in the act of receiving a legal pass a player drops the ball and it goes forward (toward the opponent's goal line), that is deemed a knock-on. The referee will blow his whistle and a scrum will take place, the put in awarded to the non-offending side.

**Penalties** – some offenses, like a knock-on are irritating but relatively minor. More serious actions like offside, obstruction or foul play deserve a more serious sanction and a penalty is awarded. From the spot where the offense occurred, the offended-against team (offendees) can kick for touch and get the throw in, or kick directly for goal and the three points it would earn them. Once they have decided, they have one minute to kick and may not change their minds.

**Playing Advantage** – the purpose of rugby's Laws is to facilitate a fast-moving, continuous game and with that objective in mind, the advantage law has been created. After an offense, if the offendees still have possession of the ball, the referee can allow play to carry on until a material advantage has been achieved, thus making the award of a penalty or other sanction unnecessary. Should such an advantage NOT be achieved, the referee will take play back to the spot where the offense took place and allow a penalty to be taken. A player who has committed the offense may not escape unscathed, as referees have extraordinary vision and elephantine memories and may take additional actions, even after several minutes have elapsed.

**The Yellow Card & the Sin-Bin** – occasionally players "accidentally" break the laws and, when doing so, are penalized. Repeated infringements by the same player or by the team, however, may force the referee to take sterner action. A yellow card sends an offending player to the Sin-Bin for 10 minutes during which he can play no part in the game. In all levels of rugby, the loss of a man can turn a game on its ear.

In the case of persistent foul or dangerous play, the referee may wave a **red card** which sends the player off the field of play for an early bath.

**Blood Replacements and Head Injury Assessments** – rugby, as we all know, is a physical sport and injuries happen. In the event a player sustains a cut where blood is flowing freely, he may leave the field of play to be stitched up. He is replaced by a substitute from the bench for a maximum of 15 minutes until he is ready to reenter the fray.

Similarly, with a nasty head knock (an area of huge concern these days and not just in rugby), the player will be substituted while he undergoes a Head Injury Assessment (HIA) off the field of play, and has to be cleared by professional medical staff before being allowed to reenter the game.

In the event either injury is too severe to allow further participation, the substitution becomes permanent.

# Other unique expressions

**First and Second Five-Eighths** – an expression invented by a New Zealander in the early 1900s, this refers to the fly half (#10) and inside center (#12) who stand between the primary half-back (the scrum half) and the three quarters (historically the outside center and wingers). So, I guess 5/8 is between ½ and ¾!! (If you should run into a New Zealander, please check this.)

**Hand-off** – when running with ball in hand, a player is allowed to fend off defenders who want to tackle him, using a straight arm to the chest or shoulders of the opponent. Physically strong players can use this technique to great advantage although the defender will try to tackle round the knees, forcing an off-load or bringing the ball and player crashing to earth.

**Uncontested Scrums** – in the event that one team has an overwhelming advantage in the scrum, a referee may, in the interests of safety, call for uncontested scrums. This eliminates the need for the push and shove of a regular scrum but also removes the opportunity for the weaker side to contest for the ball. The dominant team will then opt for the scrum option whenever they can, knowing it guarantees possession.

**The Mark** - A method of stopping play and winning a free-kick by cleanly catching an opponent's kick in the catcher's own 22 or in in-goal and shouting "mark". Once the call is made, the catcher may not be tackled. The game will be restarted from that "mark" with a kick and all of the catcher's (now kicker's) teammates must be behind him in an on-side position.

**Drop outs** - there are two significant instances where a team will take a "drop out" (using a Drop Kick):

**22 Drop Out** - when an unsuccessful penalty kick or dropped goal attempt is grounded in the in-goal area by the defending team, or an attacker grounds the ball in the in-goal area but comes in contact with the touchline or dead-ball line simultaneously. Play stops and the ball is drop-kicked back downfield from whence it came.

**Goal-line Drop Out** - when an attacking player crosses the goal line but is unable to touch the ball down (held up); when an attacking kick (NOT a penalty or dropped goal attempt) crosses the goal line and is touched down by a defending player; or when an attacking player knocks on in the in-goal area.

## Infrastructure terminology

**The Paddock** - a common expression Down Under that describes the playing field. Any suggestion that players resemble four-legged beasts is purely coincidental.

**The Sheds** - another Down-Under colloquialism that refers to the changing facilities (locker room) used by the players. Any idea that the facilities resemble farmyard shelters is probably accurate.

So, to recap, these are a few of the most common expressions you will hear, either at a game or watching one on TV. Topics like the scrum, the advantage rule, rucks and mauls will also be covered in the next section about the Laws, not to bore you with repetition but to show you the official interpretation of the situation and to emphasize their importance to the game.

*Bunt - Baseball; Pick - Basketball; PAT (Point After Touchdown) - American Football

# 3 - WHO PLAYS, WHO WATCHES IT, AND WHY?

## THE PLAYERS

If you talk to any rugby player, young or old, man or woman, local club player or top class international, you'll likely hear the same explanations for why they play the game: "a true team game"; "in the trenches"; "try your hardest to beat your opponent and at the final whistle shake their hand and go for a beer"; "a tough, contact game but fewer injuries than other sports"; "discipline"; "respect"; "sportsmanship"; the list goes on.

## Physical and mental health

People participate in sports for many reasons: fitness; skills development; looking for and developing friendships; being part of a team; staying young; etc. Some sports are solitary endeavors like racket sports, running, swimming and skiing. Others are team-based such as soccer, basketball, and lacrosse and, of course, rugby. Why do some people prefer team sports? The psychology around participating in a group activity is a topic for more learned pages but, simply, the idea of hanging around with your pals a couple of times a week training for and playing in a sport, at any level, is attractive and adds to the quality of our lives. We have enough stress to deal with in our everyday lives and being able to don a uniform and run around a field for an hour or two is hugely beneficial to us, and to our loved ones!

> **"A team is a team is a team.**
> **Shakespeare said that many times."**
>
> **Don Devine – Hall of Fame American Football coach.**

## Team-think

All team sports need individual contributions and, in some circumstances, that effort can go too far. Many of us have played in a game where some hot-dog soccer player who sees himself as the next Pele or Messi hogs the ball for most of the match. Many of us have played with people who have a strange inability to pass the ball, turning what should be a pleasurable weekend activity into a severe test of one's patience.

While rugby is not completely immune to such selfish behavior, there's something about the game that almost eliminates the practice of hoggishness, and compels the participants to act as a team.

The structure of the game involves all fifteen players (for a complete explanation of the game, see Ch. 2), including those selected for size and weight, and others for agility and speed. The game is designed to flow – the worst crime you can commit under the Laws is to slow the game down – and that almost guarantees that one player will never dominate the field. (OK, there are exceptions to that rule: Jonah Lomu (NZ); Johnny Wilkinson (ENG); Dan Carter (NZ); Johnny Sexton (IRE), to name but a few.) But, in general, the nature of the game requires total involvement by 30 players on the field, in attack and defense, for a full 80 minutes.

Playing schoolboy rugby as a teenager in London in the 1960's, I was fast but light, vulnerable to being taken out of the game in spectacular fashion by heavier, stronger opponents. It was of great comfort as I staggered back to the line to hear my mates in the scrum mutter, "don't worry Jon, we'll get 'im"! And yes, did they ever! Although it may have rattled the nerves of parents standing on the sidelines, the contact was for the most part fair, and the behavior, for the most part honorable.

# THE PHYSICS OF RUGBY

**"A collision is an interaction between two objects that have made contact (usually) with each other. As in any interaction, a collision results in a force being applied to the two colliding objects."**

**The Physics Classroom (TPC)**

Rugby is a highly competitive game. The sound of a well-executed tackle can send a shudder through the stands (and the guys on the pitch) and injuries do happen. People who play the game regularly accept that, as in any physical endeavor, there may be injuries and understand how proper training and conditioning can mitigate those risks. But while the game is tough and uncompromising, the players also accept that even though hard tackles may occur (and an occasional boot go astray) there is rarely malice in the action, nothing that a couple of beers after the game can't put right.

It is my belief that this is why rugby "hooliganism" is so rare. Unlike in rugby's distant cousin, football (the game of soccer to Americans) the "battle" occurs on the pitch. Perhaps the sight of 30 players putting so much physical effort into grappling with their opponents, saps the willingness of the spectators to do the same to each other. In soccer, there is physicality to be sure, but when a player writhes on the ground, indulging in a masterclass of acting designed to gain a free kick or the sanction of an opponent, it is hardly surprising that the fans rise up and start chucking things at each other. Passions can run pretty high at international rugby games too, especially when Ireland or Scotland are playing at home against the English. (I still can't figure out why EVERYONE hates England.) But despite the tensions of the game, I have experienced nothing but bonhomie and generosity and an overriding willingness to say "the best side won". You don't hear that as often in the Premier League.

## Toughness and fair play

**"From personal experience, I can tell you there is nothing more frightening than to see eight All Blacks bearing down on you with malice aforethought."**

**Don Rutherford, professional Rugby player**

On the pitch, the attitude is much the same. Sure, the tackles are hard, the rucks and mauls are fearsome but seldom is there much lasting animosity. When the British & Irish Lions were touring New Zealand in 2005, they won their opening match against a regional side, Manawatu, by over 100 points. New Zealanders play a tough, open game and their regional teams are always up for a match against a touring side but the game hit the headlines not because of the score, but because the two teams went out for beers after the game. That's a sign of character and a symbol of something not often seen in other sports these days.

## Supportive clothing

Another fundamental aspect of rugby that has a significant bearing on how the game is played is the lack of protection worn by the players. In American football, players wear sophisticated equipment, principally a crash helmet and huge shoulder pads, designed to protect players from the fearsome collisions that occur during the game. As a parent of an offensive and defensive lineman, it was clear to me that while the equipment protected my son, it also encouraged guys making tackles to take risks they might otherwise forego.

The current issue regarding brain injuries in the NFL should not be litigated in a book about rugby but the potential for head injuries obviously exists in this sport too. What observers should realize is that players are less inclined to commit hazardous tackles when it's their head that will bear the brunt of the impact. Just common sense, really. (Read: Health & Safety in Part 3)

It is interesting to note that several American College Football programs are bringing in rugby coaches to teach football players the art of tackling. This is not meant to change the rules of contact within the sport necessarily but to focus on the risks of head and neck injuries that exist even when heavily protected by equipment. The increasing number of football players who suffer from debilitating injuries later in life is evidence that more needs to be done.

# THE SPECTATORS

The ranks of spectators who show up to watch rugby on Friday nights and weekends all over the world are a varied lot. Aspiring players, former players, wives and girlfriends, and sundry interested parties pack out rugby clubs regularly, especially in the higher echelons of the game. When the TV cameras pan the crowd during an English Premiership match on a Friday night, it looks like a family outing. While families attend many sports, the combination of geography, cost, standard of play and time spent at a game of rugby add up to a pretty attractive package,

Rugby clubs exist in small towns, big towns and cities all across Europe and the major southern hemisphere nations and the potential for fans to watch an entertaining rugby game brings them out in droves throughout the season.

The fact that rugby enthusiasts in Bath and Gloucester in England, Christchurch, New Zealand or Cape Town, South Africa have easy access to games is a plus. Add the relatively reasonable cost of a ticket and the experience gets better. The cost of a ticket to a Premiership match in England runs at roughly 50% of what it costs to see a Premier League soccer match, most of which are based in large cities with all of the attendant expense of parking, nourishment, etc. The standard is just as high and the match duration, at 80 minutes plus half-time makes for a fairly early night (depending on your enthusiasm for the pub).

True, the facilities for spectators at some of these regional clubs, many of which have been in existence for decades, run a very distant second to the magnificent services one can enjoy at an NFL game. Visiting the Dallas Cowboys facility (AT&T Stadium) in Arlington, TX, I was unsure which was more impressive: the phenomenal array of food on offer (71 separate "food stations"), or the massive LCD screen that ran the full length of the pitch suspended high above the field so that the less wealthy spectators, like me, could see what was happening. This is VERY different to the experience offered at your local rugby club.

However, whether it be the World Cup, a professional club match, a University playoff or a High School game, the excitement is intense. Rugby lovers (especially those who understand the game) delight in the collegiality of the touchline, the effort on the field and the chance to talk about it afterwards.

Fan-created hooliganism is a rarity in rugby even though passions can run pretty hot. But with the exception of an occasional streaker (YES, some folk still do that), most of the action takes place on the field and good humor in the stands is maintained.

**Some rugby rivalries date back over 100 years and England vs. Scotland is no exception. I have attended several Calcutta Cup matches at Twickenham Stadium in SW London (England's National Rugby Stadium) where spectators mingle freely regardless of nationality. Now, there exists, to this day, a strange tension between the Scots and the Sassenachs (as they call us English) and nothing pleases a Scot more than giving the English a good drubbing. But despite good-natured ribbing and occasional bickering about the referee's calls, the hip flasks are shared and the bonds are strong. Such is the nature of this game.**

In the end, what today's spectator is looking for is a cracking game, in the company of friends and family, at a nice venue, at an affordable price, not too far from home.

Not too much to ask, is it?

Critical to these "wants" is, of course, the standard of the game. Spectators expect to be entertained in return for the price of admission and some matches more than meet that expectation.

Regular spectators naturally hold in their minds the "best" game they ever saw, their favorite player, or the most memorable occasion. People of a certain vintage who were watching the game in the 1970s frequently talk about the "best try ever scored", an effort against which games at the highest level are always compared. If you were there, THIS was value for money.

Watch: "Gareth Edwards – 1973" on YouTube. Barbarians vs. The All Blacks.

See also Appendix - Barbarians Football Club

# 4 - WHAT DOES IT TAKE TO BE A RUGBY PLAYER?

OK, so you think you want to play rugby? Before you run out and spend a lot of money on boots and a gumshield, it would be worthwhile thinking about the basic requirements you need so you can play the game effectively, safely and enjoyably.

## A Self-Help Questionnaire

First up, why do you want to play rugby? Is it for fitness, a social network, a desire to belong to a team, or to provide an outlet for frustration or pent-up energy? Do you have a dream of representing your country on the world stage one day, playing in the top-class game?

## Qualifications

As with all interests, hobbies, ambitions and deep-seated desires, there are tangibles and intangibles that may help you pick the right activity.

Tangibles might include height, weight, agility, hand-eye coordination, speed and stamina.

Intangibles can include toughness, determination, doggedness, bloody-mindedness, fearlessness, and a fondness for camaraderie

## More self-analysis

Anyone who wants to play the game would be well-advised to run a self-assessment test to ensure that 1) rugby is the right game for you, 2) you are sufficiently "equipped" to play the game and can avoid harming yourself (or an opponent), and 3) you join a team that complements your abilities.

In the "Art of Coarse Rugby", author Michael Green compares the typical "coarse" team of overweight, middle-aged, cigarette smoking, balding, part-time enthusiasts of the Bagford Vipers Fourth XV with the International athletes of the super-fit, hard-as-nails, impervious to fear-and-pain athletes of the Richheath Park First XV. A somewhat hyperbolic comparison, perhaps, but a useful lesson in the perils of joining the wrong team!

## Objectives and obstacles

The majority of players, especially in the United States have a short career in rugby: starting in High School, perhaps and continuing with the game in college or university. The choices after graduation naturally diminish. Depending on where you live (and that includes your state as well as village, town or city), choices for continuing participation may be abundant or very, very limited. And apart from geography, the demands of adult life can create obstacles to regular play. Not only do the needs of family and job play a part but, as the years go by, the relish with which one approaches a weekend game may start to ebb. While the beers after the game retain their appeal, the knocks and scrapes of this highly demanding sport on a cold day in November become less easy to shrug off.

However, for the enthusiast (and there is much to be enthusiastic about) the game can offer a home away from home for many years to come, perhaps for life.

## Local amenities

The more established rugby nations have developed a comprehensive structure of participation that supports the game, from an introduction in childhood, through every level of age and ability, that develops strong, young players who feed into the representative ranks, and also creates a solid foundation of part-time players and supporters who will cheer on club and country. From this foundation the game also benefits from the equally important participation of coaches, referees, club managers and tea ladies to name a few of the folks who are unsung but always present.

## National structures

**"We've lost seven of our last 8 matches. Only team we've beaten was Western Samoa. Good job we didn't play the whole of Samoa!" Gareth Davies. Rugby player, on the Welsh Rugby team's performance**

## England

In England the governing body of rugby is the **Rugby Football Union (RFU)** which has about 500 paid staff and 60,000 volunteers throughout the country. Organizing and supporting the game from the "grassroots to the elite", the RFU has approximately 2,000 clubs under its umbrella from varied sources including the Counties (the UK's equivalent of "States"), the three Armed Services (Army, Navy and Air Force), Oxford and Cambridge Universities, England Rugby Football Schools Union, and England Students, overseen by Development Officers, Area Managers and Community Rugby Coaches. The RFU is owned by its member clubs and profits are reinvested in English rugby. Revenue comes from sponsorships, government, ticket sales (for international matches), merchandise and licensing, hospitality and catering, a travel company and TV rights.

With an organization this deep and widespread, it is no wonder that England is consistently ranked as one of the best national teams in the world.

## New Zealand

In terms of population, New Zealand is much smaller than England but has a rich foundation to draw upon to create its world-beating teams. The **New Zealand Rugby** organization exists to ensure that the game runs smoothly and effectively across the country. With a mandate to lead, support, grow and promote the game, NZR manages the national teams, administers national competitions and assists community rugby throughout the two islands.

The playing structure from the top comprises the men's senior team (the All Blacks), the women's national side (Black Ferns - the 2022 Rugby World Cup Champions), the Maori All Blacks and the Junior All Blacks (under-20). There are five Super Clubs competing in a Southern Hemisphere Super League, with top clubs from Australia, South Africa and Argentina. Below them there are 26 provincial unions with over 520 clubs spread throughout the country. Over 150,000 men, women and children play rugby regularly and provide a basic structure of enthusiasm, expertise and commitment from which the stars of tomorrow can emerge.

## Scotland

Again, this is a small country but with a powerful legacy of fine rugby football that created the **Scottish Rugby Academy** to foster the development of elite level players and coaches. Through four regional academies the organization supports the flow of players into the professional game and international honors from improving, top-level clubs. There are 260 clubs in Scotland of which 170 play in leagues; about 48,000 players are engaged in contact rugby with more playing non-contact versions such as touch rugby (similar to flag football in the US).

Children can start playing contact rugby from the age of eight, mostly at clubs with mini-rugby sections but it is at secondary school age (teens) that participation reaches its peak.

From these three examples (the structures are similar in other leading rugby nations such as France, South Africa, Australia and Argentina) it should be clear that for the enthusiastic athlete, there is a clear way to improve at the game. Other variables include the determination of the player and his or her good fortune regarding playing opportunities, team mates & coaches and (a lack of) injuries, but structures exist to take a player as far as they want to go.

## Women's rugby.

A thriving and fast-growing component of the game today is in women's rugby. Long a feature at clubs around the world, the development of a strong international calendar is attracting well-deserved attention to the game.

The Women's Rugby World Cup was last held in the Autumn of 2022 in New Zealand. Played at three venues in Auckland and Whangerei, North Island, by 12 teams from Europe, Australasia, Africa, Asia and North America, the teams played a total of 26 matches in pool and knockout stages. The final, a repeat of the 2017 finale in N. Ireland between England and New Zealand was an 11-try thriller watched by viewers from all over the world – New Zealand won 34-31 at Eden Park, Auckland in front of a packed home crowd. Inaugurated in 1991, initially as an invitational tournament but now requiring qualification, the event is rapidly growing in quality, participation, spectator attendance and excitement, a magnificent partner to the men's international game.

(Due to the COVID-19 pandemic, the 2021 Women's World Cup was postponed for a year; back on schedule, the next tournament will be held in England in 2025.)

## Fitness

**My grandmother started walking five miles a day when she was sixty. She's ninety-seven now and we don't know where the hell she is.**

**Ellen DeGeneres**

Many top-class athletes, men and women, will agree that the best way to win AND to avoid injuries in any sport is to be fit and strong.

Rugby is recognized as being one of the world's toughest sports, requiring strength, stamina, speed and agility, played over 80 minutes with an occasional break for water, half an orange at half time and no rolling substitutions!

## Total Rugby

The term "total rugby" came about many years ago when the game morphed from having two teams within a team – heavy forwards and speedy backs – to a 15-man game where everyone was expected to develop the skills needed to catch, ruck, maul, run, pass, tackle and score! True, the forwards, to a man, will be heavier, possibly stronger and, perhaps not quite as nimble as the backs, but in a game where the breakdown (see Chapter 2) is a key area to excel, a player who has been tackled does not want to wait too long before the cavalry arrives.

So total rugby requires total fitness and the "senior" game is almost militaristic in its commitment to the credo of "train hard, fight easy". Indeed, several international squads have trained with their country's military units, adopting training regimens that will prepare them for the rigors of a long tournament like the Six Nations or the World Cup.

## Staying the course

Ideally, a top-class rugby player develops "power". Power is the ability to generate force quickly: utilizing strength and speed in such a fashion that he/she can accelerate quickly in attack or defense - faster sprints make for harder tackles. Power develops strength to hold on to the ball in the tackle, or wrestle it away from an opponent while on the run. Power + fitness allows a speedy recovery after expending considerable energy in a short burst of activity. Watch how the top players appear out of breath after a tough period of play, recover quickly, and then replicate that effort multiple times during the match.

In the quadrennial World Cup, each of the 20 teams participating is guaranteed four matches in their Pool, played over 17 to 23 days depending on their particular draw. That's a tough schedule.

The winners and runners-up of the 4 Pools will move on to the knockout phase of quarter-finals, semi-finals and final. For the top four teams, (a Bronze final will be played by the losing semi-finalists), that means seven high-intensity, grueling matches played over eight weeks.

Fitness and endurance play a major role in a team's success. Of course, skill, tactics, experience, management of the squad and coolness in the heat of battle will all play their part but key injuries have destroyed many a team's potential and those who can keep their players healthy throughout the tournament will have a better chance of winning.

For the player who looks at rugby as a hobby and a fun pastime, health and fitness is key too. Injuries are far more likely for players who lack basic conditioning and the game is certainly more enjoyable for the player who can canter past the opposition to score the winning try or make the game-saving tackle.

**"It's no use criticizing our tackling. Tell me how to catch them first, then we'll tackle them, all right?"**

**Graham Williams, professional Rugby player**

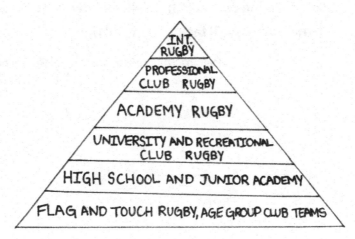

# PART TWO
# "FOUNDATIONS"

*Beginnings*

*Rugby in America*

*Pathway to the Future*

# 5 - BEGINNINGS

## A BRIEF HISTORY

Rugby School is situated in the center of England in the town of Rugby, Warwickshire, a town of 77,000 souls in the East Midlands some 80 miles north of London. The school is a special place; a 15-minute walk from the railway station in the center of this market town brings you to an oasis of calm. Centuries-old buildings enclose a broad, green area, The Close, lined with ancient trees and a Bronze Age burial ground - where games have been and still are played, and students and educators move quietly and purposefully in performance of their daily tasks.

The School, founded in the 16th Century, is one of the top private schools in England, famous not just for the invention of the game of rugby, but for turning out legions of highly-educated students who have benefited from the holistic education offered by the school for the last 450 years.

The environment in which the students study encourages learning, contemplation, and healthy activity, including plenty of sports.

Relatively unchanged since 1823, the Close, a large open area of some seven acres surrounded by the buildings that comprise the school and its residential houses, looks ready for physical activity. Close your eyes and you can imagine the tumult of the games of football played there 200 years ago: School House versus the rest of the School, hundreds of boys organized in their tactical positions by the senior students, those masters of the game, ready for the fray.

At that time there were no written rules for football, at least none that were sanctioned by the school's administration - the boys themselves defined the terms. Legend has it that a Headmaster of Rugby School, Dr. Thomas Arnold disapproved of this particular event even though he was a major proponent of physical exercise as a contributor to the well-being of his students.

**"What absurdity is this? You don't mean to say that those 50 or 60 boys, many of them quite small, are going to play that huge mass opposite?"**

**Thomas Hughes, novelist, "Tom Brown's Schooldays"**

The football played in the early 19th century involved large teams of boys, whose task was to kick the ball toward their opponent's goal. Only feet were involved, "hacking" being the term that describes booting the ball downfield as hard as possible. Injuries were commonplace but participation was mandatory and the boys, for the most part, pitched in enthusiastically. The objective was to kick the ball into the opponent's goal area and touch it down, which would give you the right to "try" and kick the ball through the posts. Hence the expression - a try. No points were awarded for touching the ball down, only a successful kick - a "goal" - would be rewarded. It was later in the century that points would be earned for both the touching down of the ball and the subsequent, successful kick.

Time allotted for the game was 5 days, or only 3 if no goals had been scored.

So rules did exist, but they were rudimentary, created and followed by the players themselves. Woe betide a fellow who may chance to cheat - the game's the thing.

But one day, in 1823, the game did change, when William Webb Ellis, some 16 years old and in his seventh year at the school (so he must have been aware of the rules), decided to catch the ball **and run with it**, an act that was decidedly against the grain. Rumor has it that Mr. Ellis, being a cricketer, may have been bored by the game and decided to shake things up. His intentions and the immediate response to his flagrant abuse of the rules are unknown but from this point on, the game played at Rugby changed direction and gradually evolved into the sport we know today.

## Dr. Thomas Arnold - Headmaster of Rugby School 1828-1842

Concurrent with the early development of the game of rugby was the stewardship of the School by Dr. Thomas Arnold, perhaps the most influential in a long line of illustrious Headmasters.

During his tenure, Dr. Arnold instigated an ethos in the school of "First, religious and moral principle; second, gentlemanly conduct; third, academic ability." Dr. Arnold was also a strong proponent of development in New Zealand and Australia and the "new" game of rugby football was exported there by Rugby School alumni.

Later in the 19th century, the famous novel depicting life at Rugby (Tom Brown's Schooldays, by Thomas Hughes) was translated into French and read by a young Pierre de Coubertin. Inspired by what he had read, de Coubertin visited the School several times in the 1880s and concluded that organized sports could be used to raise aspirations and improve the behavior of young people. From this knowledge, his vision for organized amateur athletics grew, culminating in the first modern Olympic games in Athens, in 1896.

## Development of the game around the world

Former students from the school enthusiastically introduced the game to other institutions in England, notably Cambridge University which fielded its first side in 1839, adopting the "Cambridge Rules" written by a Mr. Arthur Pell. 30 years later the first Rugby

Football Union in England was founded (in a pub, naturally), followed in 1871 by the first international match played between England and Scotland (including 10 players that had attended Rugby School). The first British tour overseas took place in 1888, to Australia and New Zealand, setting in motion an historic relationship between the mother country and its colonies via sport that exists to this day (even if the colonial relationship itself doesn't).

## International competition & other important developments

England Rugby's annual competition with Scotland (today held during the Six Nations Rugby Tournament) - was named the Calcutta Cup in 1879 when the Calcutta Rugby Club in India offered a trophy to the winner. Regular international competition was expanded to include Wales and Ireland before the end of the 19th century and grew again in 1910 to include France, in a tournament renamed the Five Nations. Italy's inclusion made it the Six Nations 90 years later in 2000, and the scope of this annual competition persists to this day, representing the pinnacle of Northern Hemisphere rugby.

Of course, the Southern Hemisphere, with its 8 World Cup wins out of 9 since 1987 also has a rich tradition of top-class rugby. As mentioned, the introduction of rugby to Australia, New Zealand and South Africa came in the 1870's, a few years before the first international tour from England in 1888 (NZ and Australia) and 1891 (South Africa). The game was also spreading to other parts of the hemisphere: Argentina started playing in the 1870's, Fiji in the 1880's and Samoa and Tonga in the early 20th century.

## Breakthrough events

Two major events occurred in the second half of the 20th century that transformed the game: the inauguration of the **Rugby World Cup** in 1987, jointly hosted by Australia and New Zealand; and, in 1995 the start of **the professional era** sanctioned by the International Rugby Board (the predecessor to today's World Rugby organization).

(A closer look at the RWC and other major tournaments is provided in Chapter 12)

## The Professional Era

Establishment of the Professional game had a profound impact on rugby across the globe. For many years, rising standards of fitness, strength and technique had put increasingly heavy demands on the hours amateur players needed to dedicate to their sport. Working 9 to 5, five days a week and playing an international or top club match on Saturday became increasingly burdensome. At the same time, the rising popularity of the game as a spectator sport, enhanced by broader TV coverage and the development of national federations, was putting a lot of money into the game, something the players felt they deserved to share.

Ultimately, despite different rates of progress towards full-time, professional participation around the world, the presence of the amateur player at the highest level of the game was phased out, and one-by-one, National Boards complied. From 1995 onward, top players could contemplate a career in rugby, playing full-time, earning a salary, paying additional attention to training, health and nutrition. Today, professional clubs around the world develop players who, to mere mortals, are astonishingly fit, uncommonly strong and exceptionally skilled. Professional rugby has become a game that bears only a passing resemblance to its origins at Rugby School in 1823.

**"Never tell a young person that anything cannot be done. God may have been waiting centuries for someone ignorant of the impossible to do that very thing."**

G.M. Trevelyan

# 6 - TODAY - RUGBY IN AMERICA

According to World Rugby's website, approximately 10 million people worldwide play rugby today. In front of 500 million fans, the game is played in 128 countries registered with the international organization, enjoying an accelerated surge in interest since Rugby Sevens were reintroduced to the Olympic Games at Rio in 2016.

This is a game that has a massive worldwide following.

## Organization

USA Rugby is responsible for the management and growth of the game of rugby union in the United States and for the promotion of America's international participation. Founded in 1975, USAR has been a member of World Rugby and its predecessor organization since 1987 and administers the game across all of its components of men's and women's rugby: youth/high school; universities; clubs, amateur and professional.

Given the size of America's population, the country's overall engagement in sports, and the size of the economy, the level of participation in rugby has been relatively modest so far, but has been enjoying rapid growth (especially in the women's game) for several years. From the latest statistics available (no doubt distorted by the COVID-19 pandemic), an estimated 130,000 players are registered with USA Rugby, and several millions "follow" the game.

There are approximately 3,200 clubs nationwide, comprising 1,200 high school teams, 900 college teams, 700 senior club sides and 400 youth teams.

At the elite level of the game, USA Rugby administers the national teams for men and women: Senior 15's; Seven-a-Side; and Under-20 15's.

## Elite Rugby

The expression "Elite Rugby" has nothing to do with birthright or money, but describes the pinnacle of the global game, where the finest players in the world meet on the pitch representing club and country.

A glance at the roster of teams selected for the 2023 Rugby World Cup offers powerful evidence of how the game has spread internationally in the last 200 years. From its colonial beginnings across the British Empire, rugby has been adopted as a major sport in many countries in Europe, Africa, Asia, Latin America and the Pacific. And while the game may still be dominated by some of the original playing nations (the 9 World Cup tournaments so far, have been shared among just four teams: New Zealand (3), Australia (2), South Africa (3), England (1)), membership in the World Rugby family is steadily expanding and new teams will surely achieve success in the years to come.

## Success Factors

Whether a country can succeed in rugby depends on a number of factors (although not necessarily size of population - look at New Zealand's success rate), including:

**Experience** (playing history); **depth** (starting young; a national network of clubs); **competition** (national organizations holding annual competitions); **investment** (availability of national, regional and local support); and **community support** (parents; pitches; referees & line judges; sandwich makers; transportation).

All of these factors combine to provide the foundation on which a successful national program can be built.

Countries around the world differ in their approach to rugby, driven by tradition, experience, resources and competition. For example:

Countries like New Zealand and South Africa have long, rich traditions and little competition from other sports;

England, (the home of the sport) has tradition and experience but more competition from soccer;

America has plenty of talent, but a geographically fragmented tradition and a lot of competition from other sports.

Ireland, recently promoted to #1 in the world after winning a series 2-1 against the All Blacks in New Zealand, has a long rugby tradition and a small professional club league which concentrates top talent. Add the intangibles of sports psychology and the world rugby rankings make sense.

At the beginning of 2023: Ireland ranks #1; France #2; New Zealand #3; South Africa #4; England #5 and the USA at #19. (France has achieved the #2 ranking with their Grand Slam performance at the 2022 Six Nations, impeccable timing given they are hosting the Rugby World Cup in 2023).

## Communities

In the more established rugby-playing countries, the foundation of rugby lies at the community level, whether it be at school or in a local club. Ideally, and this is the foundation in countries such as England, France, South Africa and New Zealand, the local RFC (Rugby Football Club) is where the game starts, where kids learn their basic skills, move up through age-group rugby, aspiring to play for the club's senior teams one day. Depending on the size and resources of the community, opportunities to play will occur alongside opportunities to support the club in other ways. Ideally, the club is not just a few guys throwing a ball around on a Saturday afternoon but a meeting place for families to spend time in their community, engaged in a variety of pursuits.

## So what's going on in America?

While rugby clubs are the foundation of the game in England and France, that is not the case in the US. There are a lot of clubs around the country and with the advent of Major League Rugby (MLR) there are opportunities for elite athletes to play professional rugby and hone their skills for the international game. However, the infrastructure is complicated and distances are considerable so for the "weekend warrior" who wants to play and improve, the opportunities appear to be less than in other countries.

A lot of young boys, and increasingly girls, get their first taste of rugby at school and in the youth programs found in some parts of the US. The game is increasingly popular for its physical commitment, plus its reputation for fair play, mutual respect and teamwork but programs at local RFCs are in their infancy. On graduation from high school, players may have the opportunity at university or college but it is after graduation that the need for a strong club culture again comes into focus. Also, someone who does not attend college may struggle to find a strong rugby network in his or her area, and that talent may never develop.

**RWC**

**+**

**National Team**

**+**

**Professional Club Sides**

**+**

**Divisional Club Rugby - League Play**

**+**

**Local Rugby Clubs - Elite College Teams**

**+**

**High School Teams - University Rugby Clubs**

**+**

**Youth/Age Group Rugby - Flag (Touch) Rugby (no tackle)**

The pyramid provides a simple view of how rugby "talent" can progress, highlighting the route a dedicated player might expect to take to the pinnacle of the game.

In a highly developed national rugby structure, the young player can be expected to be challenged by an increasingly better standard of play, requiring greater fitness and commitment for each step of the pyramid. It is here that the opportunity to earn a living as a rugby player emerges - highly competitive, of course, but the opportunities exist.

In the absence of such a structure, the young player can run into dead ends at various stages of his/her progression, limiting potential and a meaningful pipeline of talent available to the higher levels of the game.

# HIGH SCHOOL & YOUTH PROGRAMS

Due to the scarcity of local (non-school) clubs, and the strong competition from a host of other sports in the US, the most likely place a young girl or boy will discover rugby is at High School. However, in recent years, enterprising and enthusiastic adults have created opportunities to introduce and develop a youth game, targeted at pre-High School players.

But it would be a mistake to ignore the most profound influence on child/teen participation in sports ..................

# MOTHERS

It is fair to say that Mothers hold the whip hand when it comes to deciding who-plays-what in the family. Sure, Dads might want their kids to follow in their sporting footsteps but Mothers will need to be satisfied that programs are well-run, well-resourced and have coaches that the kids like and can respect.

Critical, of course, is the issue of safety which is more comprehensively addressed in Chapter 11. Contact sports, especially football, ice hockey and rugby are under the microscope for how they protect the players.

**One fundamental difference between American Football and Rugby covers who can tackle whom, and when. The ONLY person who can be tackled is the player carrying the ball - blocking other players is NOT allowed. Once the player has been brought to ground, the tackler must release the ball carrier and, beyond the rules of the Ruck and Maul (Chapters 2 & 9), no further "tackling" is allowed. Rugby is a game of CONTACT AVOIDANCE as much as possible; the absence of blocking reduces the number of contacts, and hence the potential for injury.**

Connected closely to the issue of safety is a fear of litigation, as experienced in American Football in the US and Rugby in Europe. The issue at hand is concussions: how they occur (are the Laws adequately protecting the players?); how they are dealt with at the time (during the game and in the post-game recovery period); and what plans can be made available for long-term treatment, care and financial support.

The focus on personal safety is changing the game to the benefit of all and should provide reassurance to Mothers (and Fathers) that their kids will benefit from all of the positives of rugby without exposing them to unnecessary risk.

## Rugby or Football?

For the most part, American Football dominates the sporting scene in schools. From a young player's perspective, rugby compares well to football in terms of action and participation. Compare actual playing time (ball in motion) and rugby fares well (American Football averages less than 10% "ball in motion" compared to 40-45% in rugby). Playing on an offensive or defensive squad in football can mean long periods of inactivity. Rugby, on the other hand, consists of two 40-minute halves of continuous play, halted only by the referee's whistle for infringements, scores or injuries, with a strong emphasis on "continuous" (see Chapter 9 - Referees). Also, while football is heavily scripted, rugby encourages creativity and spontaneity, each of the players relying on and collaborating with his or her teammates, responding to the ever-changing flow of the match.

## Touch/flag Rugby

The development of youth programs in America is providing another entry point to the game: today, a player might be able to participate in Under-6, Under-8, Under-10, Under-12 and Under-14 programs before entering High School, depending on where he or she lives. Starting with an emphasis on ball-handling and running, with tackling only being introduced at Under-12, young boys and girls can experience the joy of the game without issues of size and speed being a factor. And once tackling is introduced, a careful step-by-step approach teaches the safe way to bring down an opponent right from first contact.

**When I played High School rugby in SE England our team, while successful, often ran into other teams which fielded very large people. One school in our Under-16 season had a 215-pound No. 8 who, when he got the ball, made the ground shake nearly as much as our knees. However, as any good coach will affirm, "the bigger they are, the harder they fall" and when three of us 125-pound saplings combined to bring him down, it was a while before he got up again. It's just gravity, really.**

As a result, High School rugby now benefits from a growing population of players, with some experience, coming in at 9th Grade, supported by an increasing number of experienced American adults on the coaching staff, and foreign-born players coming in from overseas. Due to these factors, the game has enjoyed remarkable growth in scope and quality over the last 10-15 years and with the right support will continue to develop.

In Connecticut, for example, High School teams can expect to play 6 to 8 games each Spring, with more if they qualify for a playoff tournament. Played in the spring season rugby has not interfered with American Football programs and with similar skills and an emphasis on all-round conditioning, arguably acts as a powerful complement to the American game.

## The Inner-City opportunity

There are also fast-growing programs around the country that focus on Inner-City kids, a segment of the population that often is neglected in terms of after-school programs. In Connecticut, programs including PlayRugbyUSA (started in New York) and the City of Bridgeport Rugby Alliance (COBRA) encourage inner-city youth to learn the rudiments of rugby, not just for the exercise that the game provides but also the emphasis on teamwork and mutual dependence that are valuable life lessons for anyone.

Local coaches such as Marc Downes with his considerable rugby resume, have attracted funding to create these programs, looking to develop talent, and provide a constant stream of players who know how to play and who may come back and coach later in their careers as a way of giving back.

Marc's considerable experience playing and coaching rugby is of enormous benefit to the game, both for players at the University level but also for kids looking to get started and develop some skills.

### Profile: Marc Downes - assistant forwards coach, Yale University

**Recruited to Harlequins RFC (London) U-19 Academy 1981**

**Harlequins U-21 Jaguars, 1st & 2nd XV 1981-1987**

**Esher Rugby Club 1987-1989**

**Powerhouse Rugby Club (Australia) - 1989-1991**

**Fairfield Rugby Club Coach - 2010 - present**

**Fairfield University Rugby D1 Forward/Set piece Coach - 2014 - 2022**

## The Challenges

Dependence on local schools for the facilities to play rugby constrains a critically important component of rugby development in America. School facilities often support a number of sports and do not have the flexibility to act as a community center that can offer established and continuous support for any particular activity.

For organizations that field teams, proper facilities to shower and change, gather for meetings, hold practices and store equipment are essential to developing a feeling of belonging and team unity, as well as offering to spectators a tangible target for their support.

Another challenge is finding enough qualified coaches to offer a meaningful learning experience. Beyond running and passing, the critical skill is learning how to tackle, in a manner safe for both players - now an essential part of rugby team development. In the absence of a formal national structure that embraces coaches and referees as well as teams, the game, for now, depends on the enterprise and effort of individuals.

## PlayRugbyUSA

Wil Snape-Rogers, Executive Director of PlayRugbyUSA is a passionate supporter of grass-roots programs for rugby, especially in under-served communities.

With long experience in the game of rugby - playing for Northampton Saints in England; 5 years of coaching with the USA's women's national team; and coaching New York youth programs - Wil sees the immense value of rugby to otherwise neglected communities in America. Rugby builds connections.

PlayRugbyUSA started offering weekend rugby programs in 2003 to homeless youth in Brooklyn, NY. The programs represented a different vehicle for addressing the socio-economic challenges faced by so many of America's young people, through a new sport.

PlayRugby USA's three main programs have introduced more children to rugby than any other US organization offering development of character and skills along with mental and physical exercise. These are powerful attributes that all American youth can benefit from.

**After-School Enrichment** programs for intermediate and middle-school kids that offer an introduction to the game in a safe - flag rugby only, no tackling - and nurturing environment;

**PlayRugby Academy NY** where tackling is introduced from 12 years on up in a diverse and inclusive community where social and emotional development run hand-in-hand with development of rugby-playing skills;

**Train the Trainer** rugby programs. where public school coaches can learn how to coach rugby and start rugby programs in their community.

**At its peak, these programs have introduced approx. 2,000 kids to the game in a single year and PlayRugbyUSA believes this can be replicated in cities and larger communities throughout the US.**

To keep pace with developments elsewhere and to mount a powerful challenge to the rugby Superpowers in 2031 and 2033, America needs to embrace an equally powerful series of objectives. USARugby needs to develop a national organization with coaches and management in major centers throughout the US based on:

Funding - through events and grants and national funding sponsorships

Fields - dedicated space to play in all communities

Regional centers - coordinating local strengths and needs

Coaches - qualified, dedicated people engaged in their communities

Players - build it, and they will come!

Organized competition - especially for new, expanding girls' teams.

# UNIVERSITY RUGBY

Very few of America's 900 universities that field a rugby team have the experience that the University of California - Berkeley (Cal) brings to the game. Introduced over 140 years ago in the late 1800s, influenced by the growing diaspora of rugby enthusiasts from England, rugby initially tussled with American football as a preeminent sport at Cal, benefitting when football was shelved by universities at the beginning of the 20th century due to excessive violence, but losing ground when changes in the rules made football a "safer" sport from 1914 onwards.

Established as a Varsity sport for the last several decades, Cal has won 33 National Collegiate Championships since the competition was established in 1980, cementing a reputation as one of the leading college teams in the nation and as a regular provider of players to the national team, the USA Eagles.

The USA Eagles connection runs deep in the Cal Rugby organization. Jack Clark, a former player and coach for the national squad has been Cal's Head Coach since 1984 and has seen 50 of his players earn national honors. Associate Head Coach, Tom Billups has coached both the USA Eagles 15-a-side and 7-a-side teams, earned 69 caps playing for the US in both disciplines and has also played pro rugby in England & Wales.

These two coaches represent a strength and depth in coaching that compares favorably with any rugby organization in the world.

### Profile: Jack Clark - UC Berkeley Head Coach

**UC Berkeley Head Coach - 1984-present**

**USA National Team player - lock forward - 1979/80**

**Collegiate All- American Team Head Coach - 1985-92**

**USA National Team (USA Eagles) Head Coach - 1993-99**

### Profile: Tom Billups - UC Berkeley Associate Head Coach

**UC Berkeley Associate Head Coach - 1999-present**

**USA National Team player (7's) - hooker - 1989/93 (25 caps)**

**USA National Team Player (15's) - 1993/99 (44 caps)**

**Blackheath Rugby Club, London - 1996/97**

**Harlequins Rugby Club, London - 1997/99**

**Neath RFC and Pontypridd, Wales - 1999/2000**

**USA National Team Head Coach - 2001/06**

## The Season:

During the summer months, players are expected to maintain high levels of personal fitness following 12-week programs for strength and conditioning designed by the coaching staff. While not expected to be in match-ready condition, Cal's coaching staff firmly believes that superior conditioning is the best way for players to avoid injury. By mid-August, the team is back on campus for organized, team-based training, ready for the season. Typically, the Fall season revolves around 7-a-side competition while the 15s season starts in the New Year.

The regular 15s season, where Cal competes with teams from the Western States, lasts from January to May, with playoffs leading to Nationals potentially extending the season into June. (Cal's record in the 2021/22 year was 13-1, the only loss coming in the semi-final of the West Region Nationals at the end of the season.)

In Rugby 7s, which Cal plays in the Fall, the team won both of the major tournaments it entered in 2021., the West Coast Collegiate 7s and the PAC Rugby 7s Championship.

## Local youth development

For many years, Cal has organized a summer Rugby camp for kids of all ages and abilities, taking place at the facility in Berkeley for a long weekend in July. After a hiatus due to COVID, the Camp in 2022 represents the 26th time the event has been held. Last time out, over 160 kids from 10 countries and 9 states attended, offering not just an opportunity to learn the game and develop skills, but also a chance to meet new people from all walks of life. Teamwork and friendship are major foundations of the game of rugby.

## Challenges for players leaving University

As at many universities around the country, members of Cal's rugby team are expected to train hard and dedicate themselves to the fitness and skills required to maintain Cal's top-flight rugby reputation. However, they are students first, benefitting from Cal's elite status as a seat of learning and requiring a primary focus on academics.

At graduation, players on the Cal team have a choice of where to direct their ambitions: using the degree they have gained at one of the finest universities in America to get a first-class job, or to pursue a career in rugby.

The recently introduced Collegiate Draft offers aspiring rugby players a chance to join a professional team in the US and, as in many other major US sports, this could prove to be the most natural route for America's best to rise to the top.

One disadvantage, however, is the age gap: many top-flight American players are starting their professional career in their early twenties, having experienced the lion's share of their competition through scholastic and intercollegiate rugby. Their counterparts in the UK, France and Southern Hemisphere nations have probably been part of a professional rugby organization since 17 years old (and possibly earlier), playing and training with the best in the business, developing the skills and experience that the international game requires.

The advantage for American players taking this route lies in their achievement of a degree, an insurance policy against the uncertainties of a professional sports career.

# RUGBY CLUBS

For the majority of America's men and women, any further enjoyment of the game of rugby after High School or University will be at a local rugby club.

There are 18 geographic regions in the United States covering the 48 contiguous states and Alaska. Each region has a Rugby Football Union responsible, to varying degrees for the administration and management of the game within its geographic borders.

## A Regional Example

In the New England Rugby Football Union (NERFU), the organization covers rugby in New Hampshire, Massachusetts, Connecticut, Rhode Island, Maine and Vermont. Formed in the 1970s, the union was formed to provide cohesion between clubs in the region that had been playing rugby for many years.

 Initially, NERFU was responsible for all rugby in the region, comprising Youth & High School, University and Clubs, but that structure has changed over the years. State organizations took over the management of Youth and HS rugby several years ago and Universities followed suit, preferring to compete in Conferences along the NCAA model.

It is hard to see how a fragmented organizational structure is helpful for the sport: it is arguable that the Conference system does not encourage as much competition as a strictly regional system might provide but the recent consolidation of rugby conferences into the National Collegiate Rugby system (see University Rugby - pp. 47) might help improve the situation.

Currently, NERFU has approximately 80 member clubs, offering a rich environment for competitive rugby in the New England region. True, COVID-19 hurt momentum - some clubs had 3 full teams pre-COVID but now field only 2 and have concerns about being able to last a full season. On the other hand, the Women's game is growing rapidly with 3 or 4 new club teams recently launched in Newport, RI, for example. There are also new teams in New Hampshire and the re-launch of a club in Springfield, MA. There is growth reappearing throughout the region, including in youth rugby but that growth is uneven. The Men's game in the Boston, MA area is saturated, for example, with 15 clubs in the area all competing for the same talent pool.

In response to the nationwide lack of playing facilities, some groups in NE are trying to establish rugby programs centered around dedicated facilities that can act as the focus for long-term community rugby growth. In Portland, ME for example, a group is working on an 11-acre parcel of land that would provide a match pitch, training fields and a clubhouse for a Men and Women's Rugby Club. Public Private Partnerships are working on several ideas including a rugby-dedicated facility in Malden, MA where the Mystic River RFC, playing at Pine Banks Park, fields Youth, High School, Collegiate Selects, Old Boys and Men's Rugby teams.

NERFU"s mission, led by President Brad Defresnes, a 17-year veteran of the organization and a longer participant in the game, is to develop rugby as a community sport while facilitating a pathway to higher standards and achievement in rugby through regular, high quality competition.

So what role does America's rugby club network play in a world where, arguably, the main route to first-class rugby lies through the university system?

1) Providing a route for talented rugby athletes who do not attend college to experience regular competition. This can be achieved through establishment of regional centers which offer proper facilities to groups of rugby clubs without putting an intolerable burden on the clubs themselves (funding their own facilities; traveling long distances).

2) Encouraging establishment of Academy programs at the growing professional rugby level, where players from college or elsewhere can be selected to benefit from top-class training with the top players in the country.

## Monadnock Rugby Football Club - Keene, NH - Community focus.

Founded in 2006, the club fields several teams: youth Under-8s through high school and both men's and women's teams. Plus, active and past players have a close relationship with Keene State College, coaching KSC's men's and women's programs.

In a recent season, the almost 100 active team members played 10 regular season games in the men's division, plus 2 playoff games and were crowned USA Rugby Divisional Champions. The women's and youth teams are ramping up to more regular competition with several jamboree, round robin and organized tournaments planned throughout the year.

The team plays at Pat Russell Field, a rugby-specific facility benefiting recently from a public/private joint venture investment after previous spells at Keene State College and a local town park.

In addition, the club maintains a close relationship with the town through hundreds of hours of community service each year, including: park cleanups; Monadnock United Way volunteering; Community Kitchen food preparation, distribution and delivery; manual labor for seniors and people with disabilities; youth program development, etc.

# AMERICA'S PROFESSIONAL GAME

Major League Rugby (MLR) was launched in 2017 with the express purpose of developing the game of Rugby Union in the United States and providing a pathway for players who have experienced the game at High School and College and wish to pursue a paid career in the sport.

As of 2022 there are 13 clubs in MLR: 12 American and 1 in Canada. The teams are divided into the Eastern and Western Regions as follows:

East - New England, Washington, New York, Toronto, New Orleans & Atlanta

West - Austin, Dallas, Houston, LA, San Diego, Seattle & Utah

## Los Angeles

The LA Giltinis were launched in 2020 as the representative professional team for the City of Los Angeles and since then has moved quickly to the top of the game. With a deeply experienced coaching staff including hirings from Australia, the Giltinis have developed a strong team based at the Los Angeles Coliseum and with a roster of players from all over the world and a strong American core.

The Giltinis play 18 games during the regular season, which lasts from February to June and culminates in a knockout play-off competition for the regional Conference title followed by the National Final to be played in late June.

Another strong indicator of the depth of talent available to the organization of rugby in America comes from the activities of retired players like Todd Clever, currently working in a senior role at the LA Giltinis. Todd holds the record for representing his country both in Seven-a-Side and 15's rugby and is putting his years of experience in both domestic and international rugby to good use in the professional game and through a foundation he runs engaging LA youth in the game of rugby.

### Profile: Todd Clever, LA Giltinis -
### Head of Strategic Partnerships

**USA National Team player 15's (flanker) - 2003/17 (76 caps)**

**USA National Team player 7's - 2004-09 (24 caps)**

**North Harbor, New Zealand - 2006**

**Golden Lions, Johannesburg, SA - 2009/10**

Suntory & NTT, Tokyo Japan - 2010/15

Newcastle Falcons, England - 2015/16

Austin Elite Rugby, co-owner - 2016

## Challenges for the Professional game

**Team Rosters** - as is evident from the brief descriptions of the High School and University structures, the channel of new American players aspiring to become professional players is narrower than in other countries. And while there is an expanding list of first-class Americans on the list of all of these clubs, there is still a need for the importing of foreign talent.

For now, while America builds its "bench" of home-grown talent, the American rugby market provides an excellent opportunity for foreign-born players, seasoned and experienced from their years playing in England, France or the Southern Hemisphere. The new, expanding, American pro-rugby market can add a few extra chapters to a player's career in exchange for the knowledge and experience he can bring to a team. For example:

### Profile: Chris Robshaw - Loose forward, San Diego Legion

**Warlingham RFC, England (from 7 years old)**

**England U-18 team - 2004**

**Harlequins RFC, London - 2005/20**

**England U-21 - 2006**

**England XV - 2009/2018 (66 caps) (Captain 2012/15)**

**San Diego Legion - 2021-2022**

**Facilities** - the majority of the current teams in MLR have facilities dedicated to the game of rugby although they often share with other sports such as soccer. Those facilities have seating capacities averaging around 5,000 spectators which is an ideal size for a game in its early stages. Teams such as the LA Giltinis (LA Coliseum - football, the Olympics), and the Dallas Jackals (Choctaw Stadium - baseball, Texas Rangers) currently use much larger facilities.

By comparison, the 13 teams in England's premiership have an average capacity of 17,000 spectators. 3 of the 4 largest stadiums are shared with soccer clubs (Wasps, Bristol and London Irish) and 2 other facilities are shared with Rugby League teams (Sale Sharks and Newcastle Falcons). Dedicated facilities represent a key growth opportunity for the American game.

## Impact on the Game

Development and growth of rugby union in America is accelerated by the presence of these professional teams, offering a route for players to experience increasingly tough and well-prepared opposition that will mimic the challenges presented in the international game.

In common with other professional sports in America, the ranks of these pro teams will be augmented by an annual **Collegiate Draft** from which the top players emerging from the university system will have an opportunity to be picked by a major, metropolitan team.

To incentivize the teams and their owners, MLR has approved expansion of the salary cap limits when teams actively support the development of the game in their locality.

## Future Growth opportunities

Entitled **"Grassroots Development Initiatives"**, teams will be rewarded for developing Youth Leagues and Training programs; a High School Academy; and a Developmental Academy program, all designed to offer additional training and experience to the best young players in the team's catchment area.

The best is yet to come.

For the last few years, media coverage of Rugby 15s has improved mightily, but why does rugby still land so lightly in the American sporting consciousness? The country is sports-mad and rugby speaks loudly to American sporting values of fitness, action, tests of strength, speed, agility and, best of all, high scoring! Why is this not a national sport?

# 7 - TOMORROW, PATHWAY TO THE FUTURE

America, partly due to its enormous size but also due to factors such as competition and the lack of a rugby tradition, is not ideally structured to create a deep, talented, experienced roster of players that can take on, and beat, the world's best.

For many here in the US, the biggest impediment is a lack of real estate, an absence of the rugby clubs that litter the landscape in older playing countries such as England, France and New Zealand.

## Community glue

These clubs (like Monadnock RFC in Keene, NH) are not just places where kids can go and throw a ball around - although they are a great place to start - but they offer a sense of continuity for youngsters who are attracted to the game. Local clubs (and these can range in size from very small rural clubs to better-resourced urban organizations) can offer basic introduction to the sport through touch or flag rugby, have age-group teams where players can play similar-sized and talented opponents, right through to senior teams where talent can thrive and grow against tougher competition. Because a lot of these clubs operate outside of the local school system, there is no barrier to the usage of facilities which are dedicated to the sport. Such organizations also act as a community "glue" offering families of players a place to congregate, watch, play or support as the mood and their interests take them.

From everyone's perspective, the ability to hang out after a game and enjoy a cup of tea or a beer with your opponents, enhances the sense of teamwork and community that the game itself enjoys.

## Talent development

Another positive factor of playing rugby outside of (and in addition to) a school calendar is the opportunity to play a wider variety of opponents with their different skills, talents and capabilities. A young player wanting to accelerate his or her development can only benefit from playing more rugby during the year, against a wider array of talent. A club can also provide a different, more consistent approach to coaching which, for now, may only be available to the top High Schools and Universities. The more established clubs overseas have a tremendous wealth of talent developed over years of playing the game all of which can be used to develop the next generation.

As seen in some of the professional clubs here in the US, a lot of the playing and coaching talent is foreign-born. Like soccer, that is to be expected at this stage of rugby's growth in America but, over time, it is essential for the country to be developing its own deep bench.

A top player at a University, for example, may have aspirations to continue his career at a pro club after graduating from college. For the best players there is a clear route to the pros but they have a tough hill to climb to reach the same standards as their foreign counterparts. In the international arena they will be competing against players of a similar age, but with vast experience. For example;

Marcus Smith - England's starting Fly Half - 23 years old:

Antoine Dupont - France's starting Scrum Half & World Player/ Year (2021) - 24

Henry Arundell - London Irish Fullback & England Squad - 19

These three players have been playing rugby since they were small children (Dupont started at age 4) and have grown up in a highly competitive rugby environment. America's route to success depends on the establishment of a similar structure for aspiring American players.

## A massive shot in the arm

The award of the 2031 Men's World Cup and the 2033 Women's World Cup to the US is a massive shot in the arm for the American game.

IF the US wants to compete at the highest level and maximize the opportunity offered by hosting the World Cups, a lot of time, effort and money will need to be spent in developing a more robust, coherent rugby structure. The models exist overseas - all the US needs is the will to do it.

While American rugby faces big challenges from other sports, at least it has the prestige of being the defending Olympic 15's champion. Rugby Union 15's were last played at the 1924 Olympics in Paris where a "motley group of Stanford University players" beat the host French team for the Olympic Gold Medal, to the indignation of the locals. Coincidentally, the sport was withdrawn as an Olympic sport shortly afterwards. Rugby 7s, however, was reintroduced in 2016 and has attracted a lot of positive attention with its fast-pace, and short contests.

## A wish-list for American rugby:

- Development of a network of rugby clubs which can promote the game and train players from an early age and offer to the local community something that goes beyond sport - a shared interest;

- Construction of playing facilities devoted to rugby;

- Substantial investment at the national and local levels to aid that development;

- Recognition that players may wish to develop outside of the university system and need a suitable alternative structure (e,g, local clubs):

- Steady expansion of MLR so it covers more of the country and raises rugby in the national consciousness:

- Engagement of the American public in the benefits of the game through comprehensive TV and radio coverage of the sport;

- Maximization of the opportunity offered by hosting the Men's and Women's World Cup competitions in 2031 and 2033 - a rare and powerful attraction for millions of eyeballs.

## Two critical needs: Facilities and Pied Pipers

In researching this book, a common refrain heard from people heavily involved in coaching, playing and promoting rugby was the "lack of real estate".

Without fields to play on, clubs cannot grow, and talent drifts to other activities. The long-term success of rugby depends on being able to attract America's sporting talent to this challenging, enjoyable sport. The lack in America is a lack of AVAILABLE real estate, a field or fields that can be dedicated to the game of rugby and around which physical facilities can be built.

Such development needs major investment and PUBLIC-PRIVATE PARTNERSHIPS may be the most logical solution.

The second major need is people. Not people to play - if the structure is sound, players will gravitate to the game - but people to lead the growth of the game in their local communities. Popular coaches attract players, and charismatic, energetic, well-connected coaches and organizers can act as focal points for community rugby development.

Add a holistic model that addresses youth engagement, talent development and High Performance training opportunities and a national structure could emerge making America a rugby force to be reckoned with.

There is a strong, experienced and talented core in the coaching ranks already at work with America's youth. The few examples used in this section of the book show a remarkable level of experience available to budding rugby stars. These men have played for major clubs around the world and their country, have coached at the club and national level, and have trained young scholar/athletes to be the best in the nation. They represent a terrific foundation to build on.

# PART THREE
# "CULTURE"

### ETHOS

### THE LAWS

### REFEREES

### HEALTH & SAFETY

# 8 - THE ETHOS OF RUGBY

**Definition: the distinguishing character, sentiment, moral nature, or guiding beliefs of a person, group or institution.**

**Merriam-Webster Dictionary**

Team sports are popular; team sports are everywhere. So what makes rugby special?

As mentioned earlier in this book, rugby is not a place for hot dogs, show-offs, superstars, braggarts and self-described geniuses of the game. True, there are players who have played the game at the highest levels who merit high praise, but only accept it from their peers.

The viewing public and the media reserve the right to anoint individuals as heroes of any game – but arrogance and hubris have spoilt many an image in sports and, thankfully, have little place in rugby.

To a rugby player, a brilliant run, a stunning try or a game-saving tackle evokes a modest shrug, a pat on the back from a colleague and a "come on lads! Turn and face the ball!" True, you will see more excited responses from players during the World Cup but you get the point. As Nigel Owens, perhaps the game's most respected referee is fond of saying, "this is not soccer!"

## Background

Where does this demeanor come from? While acknowledging I am no more than an armchair psychologist, I wonder whether rugby's roots encouraged an attitude centered on fair play and a willingness to share the glory rather than win-at-any-cost. After all, the game was developed on the playing fields of England's private schools and exported around the world to Australia, New Zealand, South Africa and beyond. To the young "gentlemen" who participated in those games and adventures years ago, complaining demonstrated weakness. When attending a private school in my youth, we were not allowed to play football (soccer) on the basis that it was a working class sport: a stunningly embarrassing attitude for a seat of learning and one miserably out of touch with the majority of students at the institution. My contention is that despite its origins, some of humanity's better qualities endure in rugby today.

## Teamwork - first and last

Another explanation lies in the military nature of the game. Rugby, at its most basic, has a strong sense of combat about it: wrestling for the ball; tackling at speed; pushing hard in the scrum – all feats of strength and agility that are seldom seen, or needed in civilian life. Students of military history will generally agree that you can only win wars as a team and in rugby, such coordination wins games.

## Coordination

The physical nature of the game makes playing as a unit absolutely essential. The team with the ball must provide continuous support to the ball carrier, who WILL be tackled: effective recycling of the ball is crucial. If you are outnumbered at the breakdown, you will lose the ball. If you lose the ball you cannot score. If you cannot score, you lose the game. If you lose possession, you must immediately coordinate your defense to close those gaps through which a speedy opponent will run. Hard tackles and sufficient numbers at the breakdown will help regain possession. Teamwork in attack; teamwork in defense. It never stops, for a moment (or 80 minutes, anyway).

Every component of the game requires a team of players to effectively compete – kick-off; scrum; line-out; the separate phases of play – working together.

## The scrum - teamwork in action

The most obvious example of teamwork in rugby is the scrum.

Five players (the "tight five") are physically bound together in each set piece scrum: a front row of two props with a hooker between them; and the second row of two "locks". For these five players (referred to as the Engine Room by cognoscenti of the game), learning how to bind together, to move and push as a unit takes practice and skill. Operating as a single unit, the kinetic energy of the tight five is immense. As individuals, their impact would be less than 1/5th of what they can do together.

Training for the tight five is not just about strength and stamina (although both are essential) but learning to operate as a single organism, relying on your teammates to act predictably and cohesively in pursuit of a common goal. With well-trained "loose" forwards - the two flankers and number 8 – the scrum as a unit can fulfill a number of key roles, in attack or defense.

All teams strive for cohesion and train for coordinated effort but some reach a higher level of achievement and effectiveness.

## The Benchmark

The most consistent example in the world for many years has been the New Zealand national team, the All Blacks, who have been at or near the top of the game for decades. In his book "Legacy: What the All Blacks can teach us about the Business of Life", author James Kerr considers the All Blacks from a business perspective, examining examples of preparedness by the team that can be adopted by business organizations in pursuit of sustainable success. That's how far rugby has come – from the pitch to the boardroom.

But how did New Zealand get there? Are there unique factors in the All Black's history that have created this model of effectiveness, efficiency and consistency?

New Zealand is a small country (population: approx. 4 million) that has evolved, in part due to its relative isolation, as a self-reliant, resourceful, independent nation of hard-working folk. Not long ago the national team would be picked from a population of young men plucked from their family farms, strong, tough individuals used to a life of hard labor and quiet camaraderie for whom a game of "footie" at the weekend was a welcome break from their labors.

Adding players from the indigenous Maori population whose acceptance into the ranks occurred a little earlier, perhaps, than in other countries, and the combination was highly effective (their opponents might say lethal!)

Compared to their Australian cousins across the Tasman Sea, Kiwis are regarded as quieter, more laid back, and less "showy" (sorry, Diggers). While that in no way illustrates greater potential on the rugby field, the constant success of the All Blacks makes me wonder.

## The military connection

In the US Marine Corps, new recruits are stripped of their individuality and recreated as members of a fire-team, partnered with another Marine with and for whom they will fight to the death. ("Making the Corps", by Thomas E. Ricks). That selflessness is a key element in developing an effective fighting force and the parallel to rugby is notable, acknowledging that rugby is JUST a sport. Rugby played at the highest level embraces a similar ethos – all for one, and one for all.

The New Zealand national team goes one better than "just" developing an iron-clad, team-based approach. It leavens the bread of success and international acclaim with a healthy sprinkling of humility.

## Humility

The concept of "Sweeping the Sheds" seems to be an All Blacks idea (although one imagines other teams do this too) – a manifestation of the idea that no-one is above a team-mate or the team itself; that operating as a unit is paramount and everyone must play their part, from the most experienced player to the rookie running out in the famous black jersey for the first time.

"Sweeping the Sheds' ' illustrates that culture: after a practice or a match, members of the team are designated to clean up the locker room (the Shed) of the muddy boots, dirty kit and bloody bandages. On any occasion this may be the Captain of the side, with 100+ caps representing his country, or a new player, giddy with excitement at the achievement of his life-long goal.

Either way, there is nothing that says a player is too important to clean up; that the heroes of the day should let attendants clean up after them. They are not Gods (although at times they seem to play like them). Just a bunch of well-trained, dedicated athletes who just happen to be very, very good at what they do, together.

Another aspect of rugby humility is how, in many teams, only a number appears on the back of the jersey. That number denotes the position played by its wearer (of benefit to the referee and the spectators) but leaves them nameless – just cogs in a wheel.

Young players, dressing for their first game as an All Black talk of their awareness of the great names who have pulled on that shirt, who have worn that number before. Even today's best players talk with reverence for those who have gone before and only pray that they leave the number better than they found it. Numbers are never retired in rugby – it is always hoped, in fact assumed, that one day, a better #9 or #4 will come along, worn by someone who is just a kid today but who looks with awe at his heroes and dreams of playing his or her part.

Thinking about the ethos of a sport is worth the effort, but the existence of a strong, positive culture is not the only determinant of whether a country (or club or school) will be successful. Other factors, of course, include the challenges the sport faces in its development, as mentioned in Chapter 7.

**"The Battle of Waterloo was won on the playing fields of Eton"**

**The Duke of Wellington. General, Prime Minister of Great Britain**

**"As Duke Ellington once said, the Battle of Waterloo was won on the playing fields of Elkton"**

**Babe Ruth. Hall of Fame Baseball Player**

# 9 - THE LAWS

**"In law, nothing is certain but the expense."**

**Samuel Butler**

The laws of the game, as described on the World Rugby website, are enshrined in a Playing Charter, which relates to the playing and coaching of rugby and application of the Laws. The Charter provides a checklist against which the mode of play and behavior can be assessed: the Principles of Conduct (recognizing the inherent contradictions in this tough, physical game); and the Principles of Spirit (playing to the letter and the spirit of the Laws).

There is little utility in me reciting the Laws, chapter and verse to you. Apart from boring the pants of you, they can be downloaded from the authorities at **laws.worldrugby.org.** Note: that site contains a LOT of detail. This chapter will cover the important bits and prove both interesting and enlightening, I hope. Here goes:

# GENERAL PURPOSE

As Derek Robinson wrote in his richly entertaining book "Rugby. The Laws Explained", the principal objective of the Laws of Rugby is to create a contest between two teams of equal number and constituency (although they are unlikely to be the same size and shape) that is fast-moving and continuous, with as few stoppages as possible. When successful, both players and spectators will feel enjoyment, fulfillment and satisfaction and the referee will make it back to his or her car at the end of the game unscathed. So the Laws are against things like lying on the ball or refusing to let go of it once tackled (releasing). The flow of the game should remain unimpaired and woe betide the player who through ignorance, malice or incompetence gets in the way: for him/her, sanctions await.

Furthermore, the game is designed to allow both teams frequent opportunities to compete for the ball, openly and fairly during the passage of play, with the mutual objective of gaining possession and making forward progress to the opponent's try line.

Underlying the actions of the Referee are the characteristics of rugby that make the laws enforceable and the game manageable. They are:

**Integrity** - honesty and fair play

**Passion** - enthusiasm for the game and its ethos

**Solidarity** - unifying spirit of friendship, teamwork, loyalty

**Discipline** - adherence to the laws and the code of fair play

**Respect** - for teammates, opponents, match officials

As I mentioned, the Laws in their entirety are detailed but I will focus on just a few aspects of the game that are most likely to tempt the spectator to ask "what just happened?"

## The Tackle.

**Definition: When a ball carrier is held and brought to ground by one or more opponents.**

The carrier must **release** the ball immediately on coming to ground, making the ball available by releasing, passing or pushing the ball any direction except forward. Additionally, the tackler must **release** the ball carrier as soon as both players have gone to ground.

Commonly in a game of rugby, this evolves into the **breakdown** and a **recycling** of the ball, offering an equal opportunity for both sides to gain or maintain possession. Speed to the breakdown and expertise in the **ruck** and **maul** are key elements in the game.

## Offside.

**Definition: A positional offense meaning a player can take no part in the game without being liable to sanction.**

In the passage of play, any teammate who is between the ball carrier and the opponent's goal line is **offside** and may not interfere; that is, receive the ball from a teammate or obstruct or otherwise annoy an opponent who may be trying to compete fairly for the ball. If a player does commit an offside offense, he is liable for sanction, usually a **penalty** for the opposing team.

Offside is also strictly monitored in the set-piece components of the game: the **kick off; scrums and lineouts**.

At the **kick off** that starts each half of play, **twenty-two meter** or **goal-line drop outs, penalties, free kicks**, etc. all teammates must stay behind the player who is kicking until the ball is kicked. Then, chase like hell.

**Scrums:** there is an imaginary line of offside for the players not engaged in the scrum itself that is 5 meters behind the hindmost foot of the hindmost forward. The backs may not break that line until the ball has emerged from the scrum.

**Lineouts:** for players not in the lineout itself, the imaginary line of offside is 10 meters from the line of touch. Again, players may not break that offside line until the ball is out of the lineout or a maul has formed and the referee indicates as such. For players in the lineout, the offside line is the line of touch itself, the point where the ball went out play.

Note that the player with the greatest freedom to roam about without penalty is the **scrum half**, the link between the pack (scrum), and the backs.

## Rucks.

**Definition: A phase of play where one or more players from each team, who are on their feet and in physical contact, close around the ball, which is on the ground.**

A player with the ball must, when tackled, release the ball and allow fair competition for possession. A ruck will have at least two people involved, one from each side and there may be more. However, the ball is on the ground and must stay there and be moved only by foot unless an opposing player, firmly planted on his feet, reaches in and wrestles the ball away (the Jackal). Lying on the ground and grabbing at the ball is verboten and will result in a penalty.

## Mauls

**Definition: A phase of play consisting of a ball-carrier and at least one player from each team, bound together and on their feet.**

So, a **minimum** of three players, on their feet, wrestling for the ball, making progress in one direction or the other. Additional players may join the maul **in a proscribed fashion** to assist in its progress but, if the defending team collapses the maul to slow it down, by tripping an opponent, for example, it will draw an immediate penalty.

The attacking team, if it can't make any forward progress will be called on by the referee to "use it" (the ball) as quickly as possible. Failure to do so may result in a loss of possession.

## Offside at Rucks & Mauls:

Each team has an offside line that runs parallel to the goal line through their participants hindmost foot

## Collapsing the scrum:

**Definition: where the scrum before or after the put-in, disintegrates through an unfair action by a player on either team, preventing an orderly movement and distribution of the ball.**

The scrum, arguably, is the most difficult part of the game to manage from the referee's point of view. 8 players from each side, coming together (colliding more like) to compete for a ball that is on the ground between the two. For the team that has the "put in", possession is assured unless the opposition has a strong shove and can disrupt the passage of the ball.

A pack of 8 forwards can easily weigh 800-1,000 kilos (1,700 – 2,000 lbs.) and that amount of weight and kinetic energy is hard to control. A failure to line up precisely or the tricks played by a wily prop forward can easily disrupt the occasion. Referees are challenged to spot the guilty parties (and lack of technique or inexperience are crimes too) and impose sanctions. This will probably be the most common "problem" on the pitch during a match: even players, and referees at the highest levels struggle to control this raging beast.

## Kicking direct into touch:

**Definition: The ball is kicked into touch without first landing on the playing area or touching a player or the referee.**

Players can only kick directly into **touch** from the safety of their own "22", the area between the 22 meter line and their own goal line. Any kick for touch beyond that area must bounce in play or be touched by an opponent (or referee) before leaving the field to avoid sanction, in this case, a return to where it was kicked and a lineout awarded, with the put-in to the other team.

# NOTE: 50/22

In 2021 World Rugby introduced a new variation around kicking to touch, specifically designed to encourage attacking play. To whit, if a player kicks from his or her own half and the ball bounces into touch inside the opponent's 22, the kicking team will have the throw in. This forces the defending team to have at least two people playing deep in anticipation of such a kick, reducing the number of players in the defensive line, and encouraging aggressive play by the team with the ball.

## The conversion:

**Definition: After a try the scoring team will kick for goal, from a point on a line parallel to the touch line and in line with where the try was scored.**

The kick, if successful, will gain another 2 points. Once the kicker starts his run-up to kick the ball, the opponents are allowed to charge the kicker in an attempt to put him off or maybe block the kick. If they charge too quickly and the conversion is missed, the referee may award a second attempt at the kick.

Note: that with a penalty kick (resulting from an infringement) the opponents are NOT allowed to charge the kicker. Any attempt to do so will result in a re-kick, if necessary and possibly further sanctions against the player involved.

## The advantage rule:

**Definition: A clear and real tactical or territorial benefit arising after an infringement by the opposition.**

Following the spirit of a game that insists on being fast-moving, continuous and with a minimum of stoppages, nothing could be worse than listening to a referee's whistle all afternoon. Teams will commit offenses (by accident or by design) but if the team offended against still has possession, why stop the game? Not only will the "good guys" be given an opportunity to develop their attack but they'll be given time to do it. **Advantage** can last a minute or more and will only be canceled if the team with the ball makes significant progress up field ("advantage over"). At the discretion of the referee, play can be called back to the point of the original offense from which the "offendees" can kick for goal or choose a different option.

Note: the team with the advantage can try an aggressive strategy like a cross-field kick, safe in the knowledge that if this low-probability tactic fails, they'll have a penalty anyway.

## Time-on; time-off:

**Definition: The playing time for senior matches is 80 minutes, with two equal halves of 40 minutes actual playing time.**

Time runs continuously, stopped only for serious injuries or disciplinary conversations the referee needs to have with the captains, or to reorganize the scrum process, for example. In warmer climates, the referee may whistle for a pause so players can take a water break. There is no shot-clock and the final whistle is blown at the discretion of the referee.

Unlike many major sports, the game will continue after the 40 or 80 minute period has expired, only stopping when the ball is dead (out of play). Especially at the end of a tight match, the losing team, if in possession and within one score of their opponent, will try to keep the ball in play and make progress down field. If they can maintain possession, there is no official limit to how long the game may go on after 80 minutes. And barring an infringement or natural stoppage (ball out of play, for example), there is no reason for the whistle to blow until a score is made. Very exciting!

**Recommended viewing: "Ronan O'Gara Drop Goal v Northampton" 11/12/11 (YouTube)**

**Munster at home to Northampton Saints in December 2011 in a Heineken Cup tie. Trailing 20-21 with 2 minutes to play, Munster kept the ball in play for the next 6 minutes (over 4 minutes after time had officially ended) in a passage of 41 phases. After an exhausting period of play where both teams literally gave their all, fly half, Ronan O'Gara scored a dropped goal that put Munster ahead 23-21 and signaled the end of the game.**

So there we have a modest compendium of terms and Laws about the game of rugby that will help you understand, and therefore enjoy the game much more. May I suggest that you watch some games on TV and practice yelling advice at the match officials. They will really appreciate your suggestions at the big games.

# 10 - REFEREES & GAME MANAGEMENT

## CONTINUITY – SAFETY – ENJOYMENT

As Derek Robinson states in his book, "Rugby – The Laws Explained", "There is only one judge of fact and of law during a match – the referee. The Lawbook says so. Therefore you're wasting your time if you argue with him, because a) he won't argue back and b) he won't alter his decision."

### Wisdom

As in rugby union's major competitor for global attention, football (soccer), the referee is a powerful individual. The main difference between the two games is that rugby players don't argue with the ref. or, God forbid, criticize him. If they do, they do so at their peril.

## Safety

The referee is there to manage the continuity and flow of the game: to supply detailed knowledge of the Laws (and its surprising how many players, coaches and spectators are deficient in that area), and through interpretation of those Laws, facilitate a fast, enjoyable, entertaining event with as few stoppages as possible.

Above all, the referee's job is to ensure that play continues safely. There is plenty of potential for injury in the game, especially in the scrum, the tackle and the breakdown and a firm understanding of the Laws and their application in a safe, sustainable manner is a benefit to all concerned.

## The refereeing team

At most levels of rugby, the match officials comprise the referee (on the field) and two assistant referees or touch judges who run the lines.

At all levels, the referee is the sole arbiter of the Laws, charged with observing how the game unfolds, assessing the actions of the players and managing the flow of play appropriately. The touch judges signal when the ball goes out of play and confirm whether a kick at goal (either a conversion or a penalty) has been successful. In school games, for example, the touch judges will likely be supplied by the teams competing on the field and will be spoken to by the ref before the game to establish expectations and process.

At the highest levels of play including the World Cup, the on-field referee will be joined by two Assistant Referees, fully-qualified, experienced officials who use their knowledge to assist the senior referee with his or her decision-making. That can include judging whether a try has been scored (referee unsighted) or dangerous, unsportsmanlike behavior taking place on another part of the pitch (referee looking the other way). In full internationals (and the top-class club game) the officials are connected by an audio system that facilitates decision-making with a minimum of delay and uncertainty.

For the biggest games, a Television Match Official will be available. The TMO can provide invaluable information in tight, fast-moving situations – did the player touch the ball down in the In-Goal area before his foot touched the sideline (try, no try)? Did the ball bounce off the knee of the attacking player (not his hand) before he scored a try (no knock-on; try awarded).

## The Buck stops there

However, for all of the technical, highly qualified and experienced assistance the referee has on hand, the decision rests with him, his word is final and determines what happens next.

## Challenging, consequential and controversial decisions

**New Zealand's All Blacks vs. Australia's Wallabies - Bledisloe Cup - Game 1 on September 15, 2022. Referee Matthieu Raynal awards Australia, up 37-34 in the dying moments of the game, a penalty close to their 5-meter line. A simple kick to touch and the subsequent line-out gives Australia the win. With his team mates calling on him to kick and the referee insisting he kick the ball, fly half Foley takes his time, prompting Raynal to award a scrum**

**against Australia for time-wasting. The All Blacks win the scrum and put Jodie Barrett over for a try and the win.**

## Responsibilities

In an earlier International Rugby Board (IRB) "Introduction to Officiating", the game was divided into components that provide both guidance to the complexity of the game and, as a result, a greater appreciation of the referee's talent.

The referee is responsible for and will take action around five separate components:

**The Principles** – conduct; spirit; objective; contest; continuity

**General concepts** – foul play; offside; advantage

**One-on-one situations** – notably, the tackle

**Group situations** – restart; scrum; lineout; ruck; maul.

**Single actions** – run; pass; kick; score

By now you should understand something of these various components and see how their handling by the referee can affect the continuity, safety and enjoyment of the game, for players and spectators alike. The referee, both in training and in practice, has a lot to learn absorbing the intricacies of these components, and must learn how to observe, assess and rule in rapid succession, all the while adopting a confident, Solomon-like demeanor that brooks no dissent. Woe betide the match official who even entertains the ludicrous notion that he or she might be wrong! Anarchy on the field will follow and that would ruin the thoroughly acceptable and universally recognized, benign dictatorship under which rugby is played today.

## Invisibility

A good rugby referee (and the same can be said for any sport) is one who is barely noticed. Stop/start matches punctuated by a shrill whistle blown by an over-enthusiastic rule hound are dull to watch and no fun to play in. An obsession with every letter of the law may be technically correct but can suck the fun out of any game, which is why the **Advantage Rule** is probably the best addition to the game since rugby's creation in the 1800s.

## Continuity through the Advantage Rule

Any infraction that stops the flow of the game or unfairly robs a team of possession or progress unfairly is frowned upon by the authorities and deserves to be penalized. But, if an attempt to interfere in the game's continuity is unsuccessful and the "good guys" still have the ball, there is NO REASON TO STOP PLAY. The referee has the option of seeing if a team, despite being transgressed against, can still make forward progress as if the foul had never happened. If they progress down the field, the referee will call "advantage over " and the game continues. If the victimized team does not make material progress, the referee, after a suitable interval, will stop play and award a penalty at the spot of the original infraction.

The point here is that the official has the time to make a decision that will benefit the game overall, while ensuring an outcome of fair play. More than a minute may pass before the result of the official's decision is known, but that's OK. Advantage without a real advantage means that the offenders have got away with something and that will never do.

Rugby's insistence that an actual advantage is achieved makes this a powerful tool for both fairness and continuity.

Even when foul play has occurred, the referee may allow play to continue and only come back to deal with the offender at a natural break in play. The player may think he got away with it, but no such luck.

This is, perhaps, an excellent example of the power that the referee enjoys: to use his or her judgment in a flexible assessment of the Laws to ensure that the game flows, the players play and the spectators get their money's worth.

Simply put, continuity of play in a Safe environment = Enjoyment, for players and spectators.

## Safety: (see more in Health & Safety - Chapter 11)

Referees, the managers of the game on the field, have one responsibility that goes beyond fairness, continuity and fun – that of safety.

In a game that is fast, hard-hitting and aggressively competitive, the potential for injury is not insignificant. Referees, therefore, spend a lot of their time in a game ensuring that the activity on the pitch is fair, sportsmanlike and safe.

## Critical Points

Being observers (not players) of the game, referees can only control what happens on the pitch by setting early examples and dealing with any unsafe actions promptly and firmly. Referees are expected to speak to both teams before the kick-off stating what he or she expects in terms of play. There are three areas of concern that will be top of the referee's mind:

**1) The scrum** – when two packs of eight players push against each other in a contest for the ball, the weight and power involved is immense. Any misalignment in the direction of the "push" that could involve a twisting or torquing of the neck or spine, could result in serious injury. The referee, from the first scrum of the game, will set an appropriate, safe standard and penalize any player who does not comply. The advantage rule does NOT apply here.

**2) The tackle (1)** – a legal tackle in rugby must involve the wrapping of the arms around the ball carrier. Any attempt to tackle by merely barging into the carrier, especially with a shoulder to the head or upper torso, for example, will be dealt with severely – including a trip to the sin-bin or a red-card if the action of the tackle is severe. The theory is that using the arms encourages the tackler to tackle safely as his own body (and head) is on the line too. A shoulder to the head, at speed, could cause serious damage to a player resulting in a concussion, or worse and is, therefore aggressively discouraged. Advantage may be applied if the ball was off-loaded and no serious injury has occurred.

**3) The tackle (2)** – sometimes a tackle may not bring a ball-carrier immediately to ground and the tackler, using his considerable strength developed in the gym, may try to lift his opponent to unbalance him. In the act of lifting, the tackler must take care not to upend his opponent (legs above the head). If that happens, the tackler must attempt to lower the other player to the ground safely (Duty of Care), avoiding a landing on his head or neck. If the tackler fails to protect his opponent, the referee will immediately stop play and enforce a yellow or red card (permanent sending off) depending on the seriousness of the offense. No advantage possible here: in fact, should a player appear to be seriously injured in ANY situation, the referee will immediately stop play and bring on medical staff.

**4) The breakdown** - as described earlier, a ruck or maul resulting from a tackle involves two or more players. In addition, as each team wrestles for possession, additional players may come in to the ruck or maul to lend a hand. The force with which new players enter the contest must be carefully controlled to avoid injury. Also, players are entitled under the laws to disrupt this competition for possession by using their strength to move opponents out of the way. Any effort that uses leverage on an opponent's head or neck (a neck roll) is absolutely forbidden and will be heavily penalized.

## <u>Mental and physical fitness</u>

Training is an essential part of the referee's "kit bag", both mental and physical. In addition to having an encyclopedic knowledge of the game which can be called upon in the heat of the moment with confidence, the referee has got to keep up with play! A successful game of rugby is fast and continuous. Having contributed to the continuity of the game by applying the rules judiciously, the official is now obliged to make sure that if the ball is at one end of the pitch, he isn't at the other end, gasping for breath and wondering if a try has just been scored.

Fitness training, as we have seen for players, is a deadly serious activity for any referee wishing to move up the ladder. While physical strength is not a prerequisite (they organize the scrum, not shove it), stamina and speed are essential. The top players in the world these days are first-class athletes with sprint times that would impress an Olympian. But if the referee is to ensure that a try has genuinely been scored, at the end of a blistering exchange of passes the full length of the field, he has to be there. And the top class referees can do just that.

All of the established rugby-playing nations have systems for training platoons of well-qualified match officials essential for development of the game. It is axiomatic that from grass roots to international caps, playing the game under a standard set of rules that everybody follows is a must-have. Games cannot be played without teams, or referees.

Similar to the standards required to actually play the game, different levels of officiating are expected, in line with World Rugby standards, from entry-level matches to elite level internationals. As with the players, the expectations for elite level referees are high, oriented around experience, fitness and commitment. A top level match official cannot simply keep up; a man or woman with ambitions to reach the highest level of the sport has to work very hard to get there, both literally and figuratively.

## Try this - it's fun!

In the U.S., for example, a referee's fitness standard is measured by what was originally called the **Beep test** but is now the **Yo Yo Intermittent Recovery Test Level 1**. This involves a pair of cones placed

20 meters apart on a level playing field. The trainee must run from one cone to the other at a pace dictated by the time between beeps (provided on an app). The gap between beeps starts at 60 seconds and gets progressively faster, pushing the participant to run faster until they can run no more. The Yo Yo test introduced the idea of a 10-second "rest" between beeps, making the test more like a real game, but also insisted that the runner start each shuttle run from a standing start. Try it – it's tough!

## Challenging, consequential and controversial decisions

**"Very difficult moment - Referee Joubert on Australia v Scotland RWC 2015 Quarter Final" YouTube**

**Referees are under extraordinary pressure to make the right decision ALL the time but the tumult and speed of a top-class game make that a near- impossible task. In the dying moments of this RWC Quarter Final, Scotland led by 2 points. Joubert makes an offside call against Scotland that gave Australia a penalty which they converted to win the game. He later reflected that the call was incorrect, having had the chance to see the incident in slow-mo from multiple angles - an option not available to him at the time.**

There are 21 levels (with the time between beeps becoming progressively shorter): the standard expected of Royal Marine Commandos in the UK military is a minimum of level 11 and a "satisfactory" 13. For elite level referees, the expected standard is level 18.1!

Referees have to train like players to reach the top levels of their sport. Training will revolve around off-season; pre-season; in-season; and postseason (rest) activities. Diet is also an important function of preparation and maintenance and while you might see and hear a referee puffing and blowing a bit after a sustained period of ground-covering play, don't forget the players will be blowing too! **All** of the people on the field have worked hard to get to this level and are rewarded by being selected to participate at the world's highest level. Also remember, that recovery time is the best indicator of true fitness.

One final point: when disciplinary issues arise, the referee will step in and deal with them in a cool, efficient fashion. Unlike in soccer, the referee will insist on only speaking to the captain of each side. If there has been some tomfoolery, physical or otherwise, he may invite the offender to stand next to his captain and hear the results of the inquest but no response is expected or acknowledged. The referee's word is final and whatever sanction is delivered must be met with acceptance and humility.

A good referee will develop a respectful relationship with the players and deliver his or her expectations before the game so there is no room for confusion. Players, coaches and spectators will NEVER believe in every decision the referee makes but, if decisions appear evenly balanced and no bias is detected, participants will go home remembering the game itself, not how it was run,

To be on top of the action is essential, and the referees you will see at RWC23 and other elite competitions are, quite literally, the best in the world and can be expected to manage these competitions to the benefit of both players and spectators.

One of the best investments a spectator can make at an important game is in a Ref Mike, that patches the listener into a microphone worn by the ref throughout the game. Not only will this help explain what exactly the ref has decided in the course of the game but also can eavesdrop on the players "comments", especially those in the scrum.

## Amateur refereeing

One of the resources critical to the future of rugby in the US and its ability to grow, along with facilities and coaches, is referees.

From the top of the national rugby infrastructure on down, there is and will be strong encouragement for people to get involved officiating at rugby matches and qualification courses are readily available.

What will be key to this resource's growth will be maintenance of the respect shown by players and coaches to officiating crews (even when they don't agree with the result) and avoidance of the problem that shows up in other sports, of parents and other spectators abusing and even threatening officiating crews. Rugby is great fun and the referee has the best seat in the house and many more will be indeed in the years to come.

**During my brief refereeing career in New England, I had the privilege of being asked to referee a game between the current First XV and an alumni team of former players at a Connecticut college. Youth and energy vs. experience and guile.**

**I figured I was in for an entertaining morning when the fly half for the alumni turned up dressed as a ballerina, tutu and all. He**

was joined by several colleagues in fancy dress - including a gorilla. Against a First XV of fit young athletes I feared for the alumni's fortunes, compounded at the first scrum, where a smell of beer hung over the heaving mass of bodies. But I need not have worried: the alumni ran the youngsters ragged, were up by three tries at half time, and both sides agreed that the second half could finish whenever I decided - no need for 40 minutes. It was lunchtime.

# 11 - HEALTH & SAFETY

*"In hospitals there is no time off for good behavior."*

**Josephine Tey**

## "DUTY OF CARE"

The biggest impediment to the growth in participation in the game of rugby is the fear of serious injury, a topic that needs to be addressed seriously and continually..

Rugby is a game of repeated physical contact requiring strength, stamina and speed, all of which can contribute to injury if not monitored and regulated in a comprehensive and intelligent fashion. No parent wants to expose their child to excessive risk and players themselves often have a healthy awareness of the potential for injury. Therefore, extraordinary care needs to be taken.

## Everyone's responsibility

Knowledge about the long-term effects of repeated impacts on the body has expanded enormously over the last few years. Driven by shocking details of a deterioration in quality of life experienced by household-name athletes, the world has become more aware of the risks that athletes, both professional and amateur are exposed to.

As highlighted earlier in this book, athletes have become larger, fitter, stronger and faster over time and the equipment that protects them, in football for example, has improved in design and capability too. But the more the helmet or the pads offer a buffer against the impact, the less restrained the athlete can be with his play. And that, as has been seen increasingly in recent years, takes a toll on both the tackled and the tackler.

The dilemma for players, parents and the organizations that govern the game is the same: how do we encourage, support and enjoy the game while protecting players from the debilitating effects of the tackles that are an essential part of that game.

**Keeping physically active is a key way to reduce our risk of dementia. Sports like football and rugby are loved by millions across the UK and enable people to keep active. We would not discourage anyone from playing football or rugby.**

**We must strike a balance between ensuring people play the sports they love to keep fit and active with many health benefits and doing so in a safe way. (Alzheimer's Society UK website)**

In addition to the statement made by the British Alzheimer's Society, we need to acknowledge that life is full of bumps and bruises, especially in sports and, at some level a bloody nose or a sprained wrist is an almost acceptable price to pay for participation in a sport that tests one's physical capabilities. However, no-one should be exposed to needless or casual risk and every participant in the game has the responsibility to make sure that it is as safe as possible.

## **On the field, in practice and in games**

From a parent's point of view, rugby, while appearing rough, works hard to exercise more caution when tackling. The fact that players do NOT have a helmet and shoulder pads encourages discretion when tackling an opponent.

The technique of tackling taught to all players emphasizes the positioning of the head and the use ONLY of the arms and shoulder in the tackle, working to ensure that, right from the start, players are taught to care for themselves AND their opponent.

Referees are under increased pressure to ensure they enforce the rules around tackling, especially when the head or neck is impacted by a tackle. Penalties for even inadvertent contact with the head or neck are severe - referees will consider several factors including positioning of both players (upright or crouching), evidence of direct contact with head or neck, and the force of the impact to assess the severity of the sanction. The pressure is on to Red Card (send off for the remainder of the match) an offending player for dangerous or reckless play. In addition, the entire Rugby world is looking at ways to ensure greater safety, as evidenced by the Law that penalizes any tackle above shoulder height.

## Player input is critical

Lewis Moody, a star #7 (open-side flanker) with 71 caps for England (2001/11) and a long career with the Leicester Tigers (1996/2010) was interviewed in April 2022 about how rugby can help solve its head injury crisis. A victim of several concussions during his rugby career and a friend and team-mate of Steve Thompson (Hooker; England 2002/11 73 caps; Northampton Saints 1998/07) who has been diagnosed with early onset dementia, Moody, and Thompson are high-profile examples of the attention being focused on this issue today.

Welcoming the changes that are being introduced in youth rugby, Moody insists that it is critical to introduce all of the remedies being adopted at the top of the game throughout the entire playing pyramid. Top clubs and national teams can afford medical staff, a solution not available to small, local clubs in the countryside. Directives that give clear, unambiguous direction as to the amount of contact training that can take place and on the critical issues of tackling and behavior at the breakdown, will give all participants greater confidence about the safety of the game.

## Off the field, in the laboratory

The work being done around training and playing is being augmented by research work in several countries.

Using data derived from patients suffering from blast injuries in the military, a lot more is known about the traumatic brian injuries and cognitive impairments that can result from concussion incidents. A 2018 US study looked into Chronic Traumatic Encephalopathy, a neurodegenerative disorder that can be linked to blows that occur in sports with a high level of contact, such as American Football and Ice Hockey.

These and other studies are shedding light on the topic of concussion but also making it more difficult for players to "play hurt", an almost natural response to the player who wants to stay out there "for the team".

In professional Rugby, any player suspected of a bad head knock will be ordered from the field for a Head Injury Assessment (HIA) which allows him or her to be examined by a qualified physician while being substituted, for up to 12 minutes. If he/she passes the HIA tests, the player can resume playing. However, if he fails to respond to the satisfaction of the officials, he will not be allowed to play again until cleared and will be tracked to ensure that the recovery time taken is commensurate with the severity of the injury.

Of course, at the lower levels of the game, the responsibility will fall on the shoulders of the coaches and refs who manage these games. And with greater information coming down from World Rugby about Duty of Care protocols, their skills will be greater and the game will be safer.

**One suggestion for reducing injuries has been a reduction in the number of substitutes that can be used during a game. At the elite level, up to 8 subs can be used, all of them large, supremely fit individuals capable of impacting the game. Introduction of these "impact" players in the last third of a game can be devastating**

for a tired opponent, raising the likelihood of injuries. **A group of ex-players\* have been making repeated calls to World Rugby for a change in the Laws that would allow substitutes only to replace an injured player.**

*\*Sir Ian McGeechan, Willie John McBride, Sir Gareth Edwards, Barry John, John Taylor et al*

## Leading from the front

As well as considering the McGeechan proposal, **World Rugby** is funding extensive research into the effects of concussion on players and has already introduced protocols around the length of rehabilitation required depending on the severity of the concussion, player history, etc.

In addition, the **Game On** program to promote growth of the sport worldwide now includes variations in the Laws that allow communities to organize rugby games in a more flexible fashion. For example, modifications can be introduced based on the number of players (10-a-side and up, for example), length of game, rolling replacements, tackle heights, ball size, uncontested scrums and lineouts, kicking, weight-based banding, and pitch size. Not only will these variations increase accessibility to the game but will arguably improve safety for all participants.

Knowledge has grown exponentially in the last few decades and the perceived risk to the game is that match officials and the medical staff that assist them will be over-protective of the players and thereby changing the game in an unacceptable way. Of all outcomes, that would be preferable to one where a Duty of Care is not practiced.

However, all fans of rugby, whether players or spectators, hope to see a middle ground that protects the players from these devastating head and neck injuries while maintaining a sport that offers so much entertainment to so many.

That was then ……

**1967. Playing in an Under 15 match at school one year I fell on the ball in our 22 to spoil a kick-and-chase by our opponents. Unfortunately, my head arrived in close proximity to the ball at the same instant as an opponent's boot and my bell was well and truly rung. On the sideline, treatment was administered consisting of plentiful cold water and vigorous rubbing with the Magic Sponge (an essential piece of kit in those days) and in no time I was back on the field of play. Don't remember much about the rest of the game but apparently we won.**

This is now ……..

**March 12, 2022, England vs. Ireland Six Nations match at Twickenham Stadium, London. England #5 tackled his opposite number in open play, in the first few minutes of the game, causing a head-to-head collision that concussed the Irish player and earned the English lock a red card. The English player was deemed to have been reckless with the tackle, exposing his opponent to serious risk of injury. The Irish player failed his Head Injury Assessment (HIA) and did not return to the field - his substitution was permanent. England played over 75 minutes with 14 men.**

# APPENDIX

# 12 - INTERNATIONAL AND NATIONAL COMPETITIONS

As you might expect, a game that has been in existence for 200 hundred years and that is global in its reach has a highly developed competitive structure.

Over the last several decades, each part of the world that has enjoyed rugby as an important national sport has created local, regional and national competitions that provide enjoyment for players and spectators alike.

From the embryonic international tours of the late 19th century, pitting English teams against counterparts in Australia, New Zealand and South Africa, there are now a host of major competitions worldwide that have raised the quality of the game and allowed identification of the best teams in the world!

Some of those competitions have achieved world renown and are followed enthusiastically by supporters as an indication of who ranks as the world's best at any given moment. At the club level, the clubs that succeed in the toughest northern and southern hemisphere competitions provide the bulk of the international players who will play at the next level of competition. And the winners of the regional, international competitions give a strong sense of who to favor in the quadrennial Rugby World Cup.

However, the roster of top international teams is growing every year spurred by World Rugby's major efforts to foster the spread of the game.

In RWC 2023, several other nations will make an appearance in the competition, some for the first time, including Portugal, Namibia, Georgia, Uruguay, and Chile.

The following describes the major competitions in the world and, for the budding rugby enthusiast, will offer a great introduction to top-flight rugby in preparation for play, or spectating.

# WORLD RUGBY

World Rugby is the world's governing body for the sport of rugby union. Originally created (in the late 19th century) to agree upon and govern the rules (Laws) of Rugby Football, the organization has expanded its remit in recent years in line with the development of the game.

The most public face of World Rugby is its organization and management of the quadrennial World Cup competitions for men and women, the U20s Championship, the World Cup 7s tournament and the HSBC World Rugby Sevens Series. In 2010, World Rugby became a member of the Association of Summer Olympics

International Federations, paving the way for inclusion of Rugby 7s in the 2016 Brazil Summer Olympics.

World Rugby derives income from commercial partnerships, broadcast rights and tickets sales, revenues which fund targeted rugby programs including training and education, player welfare and high performance training. In the period 2020-23, WR expects to invest over $500 million in such programs around the world.

In addition to training and education, WR is responsible for providing match officials at international tournaments who represent the pinnacle of referee capabilities in the game. Through WRs regulatory bodies, the Laws are constantly under review to ensure that the rugby values of Integrity, Passion, Solidarity, Discipline and Respect are demonstrated on the field and reflect the world we live in today.

World Rugby's website (world.rugby) has a host of information, news items and training & education modules for the interested parent, player, coach or spectator.

The following highlights the major competitions and tours that international teams partake in on a regular basis, but in addition there are often "friendly" matches, pre-season scrimmages and one-off games that take place. Highly useful for the development of national squads preparing for the big competitions, but also great for the public who get to see their heroes in action.

# INTERNATIONAL COMPETITIONS

## THE RUGBY WORLD CUP

The premier 15s event in men and women's rugby union, held every 4 years and contested by the best international teams in the world.

Organized by World Rugby, an international federation and global movement comprising 129 national member Unions affiliated through six regional associations (Asia Rugby, Rugby Africa, Rugby Europe, Oceania Rugby, Rugby Americas North and Sudamérica Rugby).

### Schedule

Usually held in the September/October time period, the exact timing depends on schedules of the first-class professional clubs that provide the talent for the national teams. The length of the tournament is usually 7-8 weeks; for the final four teams, the semi-final will be the 6th match played making squad selection and avoidance of injuries to key players critical to success.

The women's competition will be played in October and November of 2022, delayed a year by the COVID-19 pandemic, reverting to the regular quadrennial schedule from 2025 onwards.

### Format

With 20 teams in the Men's competition in 2023, each team will play four matches in its pool. The top two teams will advance to the knockout stage - the quarterfinals - 5 weeks after the first match.

Semifinals are played 1 week later with a further week's break before the Final (and the Bronze Final) take place.

In the Women's Rugby World Cup tournament, 12 teams will play in 3 pools of 4, in the preliminary phase. The top 2 teams in each pool plus the 2 best-performing 3rd-place finishers will advance to the quarterfinal match, en route to the Final. This competition will be played over 6 weeks in late Fall.

## Venues

RWC tournaments are held at several locations in the host country, giving the local population a broader opportunity to see the world's best rugby nations while allowing a total of 48 and 26 matches to take place in a logistically efficient fashion.

## Men's World Cup:

| | |
|---|---|
| 2019 | Japan |
| 2023 | France |
| 2027 | Australia |
| 2031 | United States of America |

## Women's World Cup:

| | |
|---|---|
| 2017 | Ireland |
| 2021* | New Zealand |
| 2025 | England |
| 2029 | Australia |
| 2033 | United States of America |

*played in 2022 due to COVID

## <u>Past Champions:</u>

## Rugby World Cup (William Webb Ellis Trophy) Winners

1987 (venue: Australia & New Zealand) - New Zealand

1991 (England) - Australia

1995 (South Africa) - South Africa

1999 (England/Wales) - Australia

2003 (Australia) - England

2007 (France) - South Africa

2011 (New Zealand) - New Zealand

2015 (England) - New Zealand

2019 (Japan) - South Africa

2023 (France)

2027 (Australia)

2031 (USA)

NB: Discussions are underway to expand the number of teams that compete in the finals of both World Cup formats, thus expanding the opportunity offered to nations from all over the world to step on to a truly international stage.

# SIX NATIONS CHAMPIONSHIP

An annual competition played between England, Scotland, Wales, Ireland, France and Italy. Originally (in the late 19th century) played by the 4 "Home" nations, France was included in 1910 and Italy added in 2000.

The Championship consists of 3 tournaments: Men's, Women's, Under 20.

The Championship is organized by Six Nations Rugby.

## Schedule:

Each team plays the other nations once during the tournament over a 6 week period in February and March . Given the odd number of matches, each nation rotates between 2 and 3 home games each year.

## League Table Scoring:

4 points for a Win.

2 points for a Draw

1 bonus point for scoring 4 or more tries (winner and loser).

1 bonus point for losing by 7 points or less.

## Venues:

England - Twickenham Stadium, London

Scotland - Murrayfield, Edinburgh

Wales - Principality Stadium, Cardiff

Ireland - Aviva Stadium, Dublin

France - Stade de France, Paris

Italy - Stadio Olimpico, Rome

## Championships (2000 - 2022):

England - 7

France - 6

Wales - 6

Ireland - 4

Scotland - 0

Italy - 0

# THE RUGBY CHAMPIONSHIP

An annual rugby union competition contested between the premier rugby nations of the southern hemisphere - Argentina, Australia, New Zealand and South Africa. This is a similar tournament to the Six Nations Championship played in the northern hemisphere.

This competition was called the Tri-Nations until Argentina were invited to join in 2012.

Organized by SANZAAR, a joint body created by the four playing nations.

## Schedule:

Played in August and September every year (wintertime in the southern hemisphere) each team plays the others twice, Home and Away.

## League Table Scoring:

4 points for a Win

2 points for a Draw

1 Bonus point for 3 or more tries

1 Bonus point for losing by 7 points or less.

## Venues:

Estadio José Amalfitani - Buenos Aires, Argentina

Stadium Australia - Sydney, Australia

Eden Park - Auckland, N. Island, New Zealand

Emirates Airlines Park - Johannesburg, South Africa

## Champions (since 1996):

New Zealand - 18

South Africa - 4

Australia - 4

# THE BRITISH AND IRISH LIONS

Since the first tour in 1888, the British and Irish Lions have established themselves in the folklore of international rugby union.

That original tour, to Australia and New Zealand, was not officially recognized by the Home Unions, played no Test matches (against the countries) but played 19 club and regional fixtures, also played Aussie Rules football and a cricket match. A far cry from today's professionally organized and highly anticipated overseas trips.

Since that time, a touring side (the Lions do not play any home matches) has visited the southern hemisphere nations of Australia, New Zealand and South Africa pretty much uninterrupted, except by sustained periods either side of World War I and II. Today, tours take place every 4 years (carefully avoiding the Rugby World Cup) and represent the very best of the rugby ethos: players who spend the majority of their careers in competition with each other, banding together to take on the finest teams in the world.

**"When you think that people who spent years pasting each other come together and have to bond and find a unique spirit and camaraderie that goes on to last a lifetime, it is just amazing. But this is what is needed and what happened to us. It is easier to feel it than to try to explain it."**

**Sir Gareth Edwards - Wales 1967-1978 - Lions 1968, 71, 74, 78**

## Team selection:

The team is selected from eligible players from the 4 home unions of England, Ireland, Wales and Scotland. It is most likely that capped players will be chosen but uncapped players can be included if necessary.

## Schedule

Currently, the team tours every 4 years, to Australia, New Zealand and South Africa, in order. The last tour in 2021 was to South Africa where the hosts won the series 2-1.

## Scoring:

Being a tour, the only statistic that matters is the Won/Lost result - an issue of extreme importance to both the Lions and their hosts. And while several matches against top clubs and regions will be played, it is the "Test" matches against the host's national team that count.

| Opponent | Matches | Wins | Draws | Losses |
|----------|---------|------|-------|--------|
| Overall | 660 | 494 | 32 | 134 |
| **(Test Matches)** | | | | |
| Australia | 23 | 17 | 0 | 6 |
| New Zealand | 38 | 6 | 3 | 29 |
| S. Africa | 49 | 18 | 6 | 25 |

As can be seen from these numbers, while the record against Australia in Test matches is positive, the same cannot be said against the All Blacks and the Springboks, a thorn in the side of every Lions tour that goes back to these countries. Maybe next time!

**Next tour:**
**Australia - 2025**

# THE AUTUMN INTERNATIONALS

An annual series of matches played between the premier rugby-playing nations of the northern hemisphere and their southern hemisphere equivalents.

Generally, the European nations act as host, in October and November, for games that do not involve a defined competition but count towards world-ranking points and give all sides a chance to check out the opposition they will see in the World Cup.

As an example, the 2022 series provided the following match-ups:

**England - vs. Argentina, Japan, New Zealand and South Africa**

**Ireland - vs. South Africa, Fiji and Australia**

**Wales - vs. New Zealand, Argentina, and Australia**

**Scotland - vs. Australia, Fiji, New Zealand and Argentina**

**France - vs. Australia, Japan and South Africa.**

In addition, the Autumn Internationals offer opportunities for smaller rugby-playing nations to test their mettle against the Big Guys. For example, Georgia, an up-and-coming European side, traveled to Wales as part of their tune-up for the 2023 World Cup for which they qualified early in 2022. In recent years, the USA, Tonga and Samoa have also been invited to Europe for these matches, gaining valuable experience in top-flight rugby and visiting some of the world's iconic stadiums.

## **Venues:**

England – Twickenham Stadium, London

Ireland - Aviva Stadium, Dublin

Wales - Principality Stadium, Cardiff

Scotland, Murrayfield, Edinburgh

France - Stade de France, Paris

# **SUMMER TOURS**

Most of the northern hemisphere teams also embark on summer (pre-season) tours - a time to test new, young players and prepare for the sterner tests ahead. For example, in 2022:

England - Australia (3 tests)

Ireland - New Zealand (3 tests against the All Blacks and 2 vs. the Maori All Blacks)

Wales - South Africa (3 tests)

Scotland - Chile (1) and Argentina (3 tests)

# THE BARBARIANS

The Barbarians Football Club, also known as the Baa-baas, was created in 1890 by a gentleman looking to extend the regular season (which in those days finished in March) by inviting a few players to join him in a tour of Northern England. As well as providing more playing time, it was an opportunity to play alongside players who had always been on opposing sides, developing a feeling of camaraderie that echoed the ethos of the developing game.

The Barbarians is a British rugby club with no home ground or clubhouse. They play at the invitation of clubs or national unions, the majority of their games having taken place in the home countries of Britain but players from 25 other countries have received invitations to play.

The philosophy of the club was and is to play attacking, adventurous rugby without the pressure of having to win - for the joy of the game.

Players are selected by invitation only, the qualifications being of a good enough standard and being able to behave himself on or off the field.

### The Barbarian FC Motto:

**"Rugby Football is a game for gentlemen in all classes, but for no bad sportsmen in any class"**

**Bishop William Julius Carey - former Bishop of Bloemfontein - former Barbarian, 1894**

## Barbarian traditions:

The team wears black and white hooped jerseys with black shorts, but wear the socks of the club they play for.

Including at least one un-capped player in each starting XV.

Playing International touring sides visiting Great Britain at the end of their tour.

**The Greatest Try Ever Scored?**

**On January 27, 1973 the Barbarians hosted the All Blacks from New Zealand at Cardiff Arms Park in Wales before a sell-out crowd. In the first few minutes of the game, the Baa-Baas scored perhaps the greatest try to be witnessed by such a large audience, the ball passing through 7 players' hands before being touched down by Gareth Edwards, Wales' greatest player.**

# CLUB COMPETITIONS

## THE GALLAGHER PREMIERSHIP

The top professional rugby union division in English rugby. Contested between 13 clubs (in 2022): Bath; Bristol Bears; Exeter Chiefs; Gloucester Rugby; Harlequins; Leicester Tigers; London Irish; Newcastle Falcons; Northampton Saints; Sale Sharks; Saracens; Wasps**; Worcester Warriors**.

Organized by Premiership Rugby which, as well as organizing the Gallagher Premiership Rugby League, also controls the premiership Rugby Cup, the Premiership Rugby Shield and the Under-18 Academy competition. 14 teams are scheduled to compete in the 2022/23 season

## Schedule:

26 rounds of matches, each team plays 24 matches with two bye weeks, between September and late May/early June. The top 4 teams play semi final playoffs, the two winners play the final at Twickenham Stadium in London in June.

## League Table Scoring:

4 points for a Win

2 points for a Draw

1 Bonus Point for scoring 4 tries or more

1 Bonus Point for losing by 7 points or less

## Venues:

Harlequins - Twickenham, London

London Irish - Brentford, London

Saracens - Finchley, London

Wasps - Coventry

## Championships (2002/3-22):

Leicester Tigers – 5        Harlequins - 2

Saracens – 5                Northampton Saints – 1

Wasps – 4                   Sale Sharks - 1

** Both Wasps and Worcester Warriors withdrew from the Premiership during the 2022/23 season citing severe financial difficulties

# UNITED RUGBY CHAMPIONSHIP

An annual rugby union competition involving 16 professional teams from 5 countries

organized into 4 regional groups: Ireland (4 teams); South Africa (4); Wales (4) and Scotland (2) + Italy (2). The League last expanded in 2021 to include the 4 South African teams which had previously played in southern hemisphere competition.

The teams are Leinster, Ulster, Munster and Connacht; The Stormers, Bulls, Sharks and Lions; the Scarlets, Dragons, Ospreys and Cardiff; Glasgow Warriors & Edinburgh; and Benetton and Zebre Parma.

## Schedule:

The teams are divided up into the 4 regional pools and they play each opponent within that bracket twice. They play teams from other pools once for a total of 18 matches. The top 8 teams play a knockout format to determine the Champion - the season extends from September to May.

## League Table Scoring:

Same as the Gallagher Premiership

## **Venues:**

Leinster - Dublin, Ireland

Ulster - Belfast, N. Ireland

Munster - Cork & Limerick, Ireland

Connacht - Galway, Ireland

Stormers - Cape Town, South Africa

Bulls - Pretoria, SA

Sharks - Durban, SA

Lions - Johannesburg, SA

Scarlets - Llanelli, Wales

Dragons - Newport, Waes

Cardiff Rugby - Wales

Ospreys - Swansea, Wales

Glasgow Warriors - Scotland

Edinburgh Rugby - Scotland

Zebre Parma - Parma, Italy

Benetton - Treviso, Italy

## **Championships (2012/13 - 2021/22)**

Leinster - 6 Glasgow Warriors - 1 Connacht - 1 Scarlets - 1 Stormers - 1

# TOP 14 (FRANCE)

The third of the major professional leagues in Europe, Top 14 is a rugby union league competition played in France. Club rugby has been played there since 1892 and the Top 14 is the highest division in French rugby. Also known as LNR (Ligue Nationale Rugby) an organizing body created in 1998.

The teams are: Biarritz, Bordeaux-Bègles, Brive, Castres, Clermont, La Rochelle, Lyons, Montpellier, Section Paloise, Perpignan, Racing 92, Rugby Club Toulonnais, Stade Français Paris, Stade Toulousain.

## Schedule:

The teams play a total of 26 regular season games from September to June, 13 at home and 13 away. The top 2 at the end of the season have a place in the semi-finals while the other 2 slots are decided by playoffs between the next 4 clubs. The final is played in Paris in late June.

## League Table Scoring:

4 points for a win

2 points for a draw

1 bonus point for scoring 3 tries or more

1 bonus point for losing by 5 points of less

## Venues:

ASM Clermont - Clermont Ferrand

Racing 92 - Nanterre, Paris

Section Paloise - Pau

Stade Rochelais - La Rochelle

## Champions (2021/22)

Montpellier

# HEINEKEN CHAMPIONS CUP - EUROPE

The Heineken Champions Cup (also known as the European Rugby Champions Cup) is an annual rugby union tournament organized by European Professional Club Rugby. It represents the highest level of competition for clubs whose home countries participate in the Six Nations tournament.

24 clubs qualify for the annual competition based on their final rankings in the previous season. The top 8 finishers from the Gallagher English Premiership; 4 winners of the regional pools plus the 4 next-highest ranked finishers from the United Rugby Championship; and the 8 highest ranked finishers in France's Top 14.

Qualifiers: 2022/23 competition: Clermont, Bristol Bears, Connacht, Exeter Chiefs, Harlequins, Leicester Tigers, Montpellier, Munster, Ospreys, Racing 92, Sale Sharks, Scarlets, Stade Francais, Stade Rochelais, Stade Toulousian, Ulster, Bordeaux-Begles.

## Schedule:

The 24 clubs are divided into 4 tiers of 6 clubs based on their performance in the knockout phase and/or qualifying position of their respective leagues.

The 4 tiers are further divided into 2 pools of 12 clubs which will play 4 games each, 2 Home and 2 Away (note that clubs from the same league will not play each other at this stage of the competition).

The top 8 clubs in each pool (A & B) will move to the knockout round of 16 with single games progressing to a final.

This competition extends from December to May.

## League Table Scoring:

4 points for a Win; 2 points for a Draw

1 Bonus point for 4 tries or more

1 Bonus point for losing by 7 points or less.

## Venues:

| | |
|---|---|
| ASM Clermont - Clermont Ferrand | Scarlets - Llanelli, Wales |
| Harlequins - Twickenham, London | Stade Francais - Paris |
| Ospreys - Swansea, Wales | Stade Rochelais - La Rochelle |
| Racing 92 - Nanterre, Paris | Ulster Rugby - Belfast, N. Ireland |

## Champions (2014-2022)

Toulon 3; Saracens 3; Leinster 1; Exeter 1; Stade Rochelais 1

# SUPER RUGBY

Super Rugby is a southern hemisphere professional club rugby union league that has had several iterations over the last decade or two. Most recently affected by COVID-19, the league which in the past has had teams from South Africa, Japan and Argentina, has reverted to its original New Zealand and Australia format with the addition of two Pacific Islands-based sides.

There are 12 teams, 5 from Australia - the Brumbies, Rebels, Warratahs, Reds and Western Force; 5 from New Zealand - the Blues, Chiefs, Crusaders, Highlanders and Hurricanes; and the Fijian Drua and Moana Pasifika from the Pacific Island.

## Schedule:

Played between February and June each team has 14 regular season matches divided equally between home and away fixtures. The teams play 8 teams once and 3 teams twice, emphasizing the attraction of local derbies. The top 8 teams at the end of the season move to a standard knockout format to determine the champion.

## League Table scoring:

4 points for a win, 2 for a draw, 0 for a loss. 1 bonus point for scoring 3 or more tries and 1 bonus point for losing by less than 8 points.

## **Venues:**

Blues - Auckland, NZ

Brumbies - Canberra, Australia

Chiefs - Hamilton, NZ

Crusaders - Christchurch, NZ

Fijian Drua - Fiji

Highlanders - Dunedin, NZ

Hurricanes - Wellington, NZ

Rebels - Melbourne, Australia

Moana Pasifika - Fiji, Samoa, Tonga, Cook Islands

Warratahs - Sydney, Australia

Queensland Reds - Brisbane, Australia

Western Force - Perth, Australia

## **Championships:**

2022 - Crusaders

# BIBLIOGRAPHY

The following sources were used in the research and writing of this book:

## Books:

"With a Fine Disregard ...... " - a portrait of Rugby School - Third Millennium Publishing

Tom Brown's Schooldays - Thomas Hughes - MacMillan & Co. (1889)

Rugby: The Laws Explained - Derek Robinson - Whistle Books

The Art of Coarse Rugby - Michael Green - Robson Books

The British & Irish Lions Official History - Vision Sports Publishing

Legacy: What the All Blacks can teach us about the business of life - James Kerr - Constable Books

Making the Corps - Thomas E. Ricks - Touchstone (Simon & Schuster)

Running with the ball - Jennifer Macrory - Collins Willow

The Ultimate Dictionary of Sports Quotations - Carlo DeVito - Checkmark Books

Great British Wit - Rosemarie Jarski - Ebury Press
Brit Wit - edited by Susie Jones - Summersdale Publishing

The Wicked Wit of Winston Churchill - Dominique Enright - Michael O'Mara Books

The Oxford Book of Aphorisms - John Gross - Oxford University Press

## **Websites:**

World Rugby - world.rugby

Rugby World Cup - rugbyworldcup.com

USA Rugby - usa.rugby

RFU (England) - englandrugby.com

New Zealand Rugby - nzrugby.co.nz

The NZ All Blacks - allblacks.com

Scotland Rugby - scottishrugby.org

The Six Nations Tournament - sixnationsrugby.com

The Rugby Championship (S. Hemisphere) –
super.rugby/therugbychampionship

British and Irish Lions - lionsrugby.com

Barbarians FC - barbariansfc.co.uk

Gallagher Premiership (England) - premiershiprugby.com

URC (Europe and S. Africa) - unitedrugby.com

Top 14 (France) - lnr.fr/rugby-top-14

Super Rugby (ANZ) - super.rugby

Heineken Champions Cup (UK & Europe) - epcrugby.com

New England Rugby Football Union - nerfu.rugby

PlayRugbyUSA - playrugbyusa.org

Bridgeport (CT) Rugby Alliance - friendsoffairfieldrugby.org

UC Berkeley Golden Bears Rugby - calbears.com/sports/mens-rugby

National Collegiate Rugby (US) - ncr.rugby

LA Giltinis - giltinis.com

Major League Rugby (N. America) - major league.rugby

New England Rugby Referees Society - nerugbyrefs.org

Wellington (NZ) Rugby Referees Association - wrra.org.nz

## **Health & Safety:**

The Physics Classroom (TPC) - www.physicsclassroom.com

Concussions in young athletes https://doi.org/10.1093/brain/awx350

Preliminary study of Early Onset Dementia of former professional footballers and hockey players https://doi.org/10.1093/brain/awx350

Contact sports and the risks of Parkinson's disease https://www.medicalnewstoday.com/articles/322613

Lewis Moody Interview: "How Rugby can help solve its head injury crisis" - Daily Telegraph (UK) April 12, 2022

Sir Ian McGeechan article: "My plea to World Rugby, one year on from player safety letter" - Daily Telegraph (UK) September 18, 2022

# INDEX

## HEALTH & SAFETY:

## HISTORY:

## PITCH:

## POSITIONS:

**REFEREES:**

**JON PASSMORE** is a retired businessman and life-long fan of Rugby Union. Having played as a schoolboy and refereed briefly in New England, his rugby career has been largely seated, either at home or attending matches in the UK, Japan and the US. Part of his interest lies in the enrichment of the spectator experience.

His writing credits up until now have been confined to the world of finance and investor relations but his focus now is on development of rugby in America and he hopes to be one of many new voices speaking loudly about this terrific game.

Contact the author at jon@scrumslineouts.com